초등학생의 영어 친구

리스닝 버디 단어장

2

NE 능률

초등학생의 영어 친구

리스닝 버디 단어장 2

NE 능률

CONTENTS

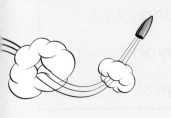

발음 기호를 배워 봅시다.

하나의 알파벳이 여러 소리를 가지고 있는 경우가 있어서, 같은 알파벳이라도 단어에 따라 소리가 달라져요. 하지만 발음 기호를 알아두면 영어 단어를 바르게 읽을 수 있답니다. 듣고 따라 하면서 발음 기호를 익혀봅시다.

★ 자음 ★

기호	단어
p	pizza [píːtsə]
b	brother [brʌðər]
t	tall [tɔːl]
d	day [dei]
k	key [kiː]
g	glad [glæd]
tʃ	choose [tʃuːz]
dʒ	jacket [dʒǽkit]
s	see [siː]
z	zoo [zuː]
ʃ	shoes [ʃuːz]
ʒ	pleasure [pléʒər]
h	have [hæv]
m	morning [mɔ́ːrniŋ]
n	name [neim]
ŋ	sing [siŋ]
f	family [fǽməli]
v	violin [vàiəlín]

기호	단어
θ	throw [θrou]
ð	this [ðis]
l	lizard [lízərd]
r	rabbit [rǽbit]
j	yes [jes]
w	want [wɑnt]

★ 모음 ★

기호	단어
a	doctor [dάktər]
e	pet [pet]
i	meet [miːt]
o	go [gou]
u	blue [bluː]
æ	cat [kæt]
ʌ	fun [fʌn]
ɔ	long [lɔ(ː)ŋ]
ə	crayon [kréiən]
ɛ	wear [wɛər]

UNIT 1 COLORS AND SHAPES

WORDS

듣고 따라 말해 봅시다.

□ **red** [red]	빨간색의	□ **rectangle** [réktæŋgl]	직사각형
□ **yellow** [jélou]	노란색의	□ **triangle** [tráiæŋgl]	삼각형
□ **green** [gri:n]	초록색의	□ **find** [faind]	찾다, 발견하다
□ **blue** [blu:]	파란색의	□ **mirror** [mírər]	거울
□ **circle** [sə́:rkl]	원형	□ **clock** [klɑ:k]	시계
□ **square** [skwɛər]	정사각형	□ **button** [bʌ́tn]	단추

EXPRESSIONS

듣고 따라 말해 봅시다.

□ A: What color is it? (그것은 무슨 색이니?)
　 B: It's red. (빨간색이야.)

□ A: What shape is it? (그것은 무슨 모양이니?)
　 B: It's a circle. (원형이야.)

WORDS & EXPRESSIONS TEST

A 다음 영어는 한글로, 한글은 영어로 쓰시오.

1 blue _____

2 triangle _____

3 clock _____

4 circle _____

5 find _____

6 정사각형 _____

7 초록색의 _____

8 단추 _____

9 노란색의 _____

10 직사각형 _____

B 다음 문장을 해석하시오.

1 What shape is it?

→ _____

2 It's red.

→ _____

3 It's a circle.

→ _____

4 What color is it?

→ _____

WoW!

UNIT 2 EVERYDAY LIFE

WORDS

듣고 따라 말해 봅시다.

□ **get up**	일어나다	□ **do homework**	숙제를 하다
□ **go to school**	학교에 가다	□ **go to bed**	자다
□ **have lunch**	점심을 먹다	□ **late** [leit]	늦은
□ **go home**	집에 가다	□ **early** [ə́:rli]	일찍
□ **exercise** [éksərsaiz]	운동하다	□ **after** [ǽftər]	~의 후에[뒤에]

EXPRESSIONS

듣고 따라 말해 봅시다.

□ A: What time is it? (몇 시야?)

  B: It's 7:30. It's time to get up. (7시 30분이야. 일어날 시간이야.)

□ A: What time do you go to bed? (넌 몇 시에 자니?)

  B: I go to bed at 10 o'clock. (난 10시에 자.)

WORDS & EXPRESSIONS TEST

A 다음 영어는 한글로, 한글은 영어로 쓰시오.

1 go to school _____   6 점심을 먹다 _____

2 get up _____   7 운동하다 _____

3 do homework _____   8 늦은 _____

4 early _____   9 자다 _____

5 after _____   10 집에 가다 _____

B 다음을 바르게 배열하여 문장을 완성하시오.

1 time / it's / get up / to / .

  → _____

2 go to / at / I / 12 o'clock / bed / .

  → _____

3 do / go to / you / bed / time / what / ?

  → _____

4 it / is / what / time / ?

  → _____

UNIT 3 FEELINGS

WORDS

듣고 따라 말해 봅시다.

□ **happy** [hǽpi]	행복한	□ **worried** [wɔ́:rid]	걱정하는
□ **sad** [sæd]	슬픈	□ **tired** [taiərd]	피곤한
□ **excited** [iksáitid]	신이 난	□ **noisy** [nɔ́izi]	시끄러운
□ **angry** [ǽŋgri]	화난	□ **outside** [àutsáid]	밖에, 밖으로
□ **scared** [skɛərd]	무서워하는	□ **spider** [spáidər]	거미
□ **bored** [bɔ́:rd]	지루한	□ **sick** [sik]	아픈

EXPRESSIONS

듣고 따라 말해 봅시다.

□ A: How do you feel? (기분이 어때?)
　 B: I'm excited. (신나.)

□ A: Are you scared? (너 무섭니?)
　 B: Yes, I am. / No, I'm not. (응, 무서워. / 아니, 무섭지 않아.)

WORDS & EXPRESSIONS TEST

DATE   PARENTS   TEACHER

A 다음 영어는 한글로, 한글은 영어로 쓰시오.

1 scared _____
6 신이 난 _____

2 bored _____
7 걱정하는 _____

3 tired _____
8 화난 _____

4 outside _____
9 슬픈 _____

5 sick _____
10 시끄러운 _____

B 다음 우리말을 바르게 영작하시오.

1 너 무섭니?

→ _____ _____ _____?

2 기분이 어때?

→ _____ _____ _____ _____?

3 신나.

→ _____ _____.

UNIT 4 BODY PARTS

WORDS

듣고 따라 말해 봅시다.

□ **eye** [ai]	눈	□ **leg** [leg]	다리
□ **nose** [nouz]	코	□ **foot** [fut]	발 (*pl.* feet)
□ **mouth** [mauθ]	입	□ **big** [big]	큰
□ **ear** [iər]	귀	□ **small** [smɔ:l]	작은
□ **arm** [ɑ:rm]	팔	□ **long** [lɔ(:)ŋ]	긴
□ **hand** [hænd]	손	□ **short** [ʃɔ:rt]	짧은

EXPRESSIONS

듣고 따라 말해 봅시다.

□ A: What does it look like? (그것은 어떻게 생겼니?)

   B: It has big ears. (귀가 커.)

□ A: How many eyes does it have? (그것은 눈이 몇 개니?)

   B: It has three eyes. (세 개야.)

WORDS & EXPRESSIONS TEST

A 다음 영어는 한글로, 한글은 영어로 쓰시오.

1 leg _____   6 팔 _____

2 ear _____   7 다리 _____

3 foot _____   8 코 _____

4 mouth _____   9 작은 _____

5 big _____   10 짧은 _____

B 다음 문장을 해석하시오.

1 What does it look like?

    → _____

2 How many eyes does it have?

    → _____

3 It has big ears.

    → _____

4 It has three eyes.

    → _____

WoW!

12

UNIT 5 AT HOME

WORDS

듣고 따라 말해 봅시다.

key [ki:]	열쇠	bookshelf [búkʃèlf]	책꽂이
watch [watʃ]	손목시계	in [in]	~ 안에, ~ 속에
socks [saks]	양말	on [ən]	~ 위에
glasses [glǽsiz]	안경	under [ʌ́ndər]	~ 아래에
bed [bed]	침대	desk [desk]	책상
table [téibl]	탁자	chair [tʃɛ́ər]	의자
drawer [drɔ:r]	서랍	doll [da:l]	인형

EXPRESSIONS

듣고 따라 말해 봅시다.

- A: Where is my car key? (내 자동차 열쇠가 어디 있지?)
  B: It's in the drawer. (서랍 안에 있어요.)

- A: Whose socks are these? (이거 누구 양말이니?)
  B: They are mine. (그거 내 거야.)

WORDS & EXPRESSIONS TEST

A 다음 영어는 한글로, 한글은 영어로 쓰시오.

1 drawer _____   6 의자 _____

2 in _____   7 손목시계 _____

3 table _____   8 책꽂이 _____

4 socks _____   9 ~ 아래에 _____

5 key _____   10 안경 _____

B 다음을 바르게 배열하여 문장을 완성하시오.

1 are / they / mine / .

→ _____

2 in / drawer / it's / the / .

→ _____

3 car / my / is / key / where / ?

→ _____

4 whose / these / are / socks / ?

→ _____

WoW!

UNIT 6 SCHOOL SUBJECTS

WORDS

듣고 따라 말해 봅시다.

□ **art**
[ɑːrt]
미술

□ **music**
[mjúːzik]
음악

□ **English**
[íŋgliʃ]
영어

□ **math**
[mæθ]
수학

□ **science**
[sáiəns]
과학

□ **P.E.**
체육

□ **history**
[hístəri]
역사

□ **subject**
[sʌ́bdʒikt]
과목

□ **favorite**
[féivərit]
가장 좋아하는

□ **be interested in**
~에 관심이 있다

□ **hard**
[hɑːrd]
어려운

□ **boring**
[bɔ́ːriŋ]
지루한

EXPRESSIONS

듣고 따라 말해 봅시다.

□ A: What's your favorite subject? (네가 가장 좋아하는 과목은 뭐니?)

B: My favorite subject is science. (내가 가장 좋아하는 과목은 과학이야.)

□ A: Are you interested in painting? (너는 그림 그리기에 관심이 있니?)

B: Yes. I like art class. (응. 나는 미술 수업을 좋아해.)

15

WORDS & EXPRESSIONS TEST

DATE   PARENTS   TEACHER

A 다음 영어는 한글로, 한글은 영어로 쓰시오.

1 math _____

2 art _____

3 science _____

4 hard _____

5 be interested in _____

6 역사 _____

7 지루한 _____

8 가장 좋아하는 _____

9 영어 _____

10 음악 _____

B 다음 우리말을 바르게 영작하시오.

1 너는 그림 그리기에 관심이 있니?

→ _____ _____ _____ _____?

2 내가 가장 좋아하는 과목은 과학이야.

→ _____ _____ _____ _____ _____.

3 네가 가장 좋아하는 과목은 뭐니?

→ _____ _____ _____ _____?

4 나는 미술 수업을 좋아해.

→ _____ _____ _____ _____.

WoW!

UNIT 7 HOBBIES

WORDS

듣고 따라 말해 봅시다.

☐ **listen to music**	음악을 듣다	☐ **do puzzles**	퍼즐을 맞추다
☐ **play tennis**	테니스를 치다	☐ **hobby** [háːbi]	취미
☐ **watch movies**	영화를 보다	☐ **free time**	여가시간
☐ **take photos**	사진을 찍다	☐ **read** [riːd]	(책 등을) 읽다
☐ **play computer games**	컴퓨터 게임을 하다	☐ **camera** [kǽmərə]	카메라

EXPRESSIONS

듣고 따라 말해 봅시다.

☐ A: What do you like to do in your free time?
　(너는 여가시간에 무엇을 하는 것을 좋아하니?)
　B: I like to play computer games. (나는 컴퓨터 게임 하는 것을 좋아해.)

☐ A: How about listening to music? (음악 듣는 게 어때?)
　B: That sounds good. (좋은 생각이야.)

WORDS & EXPRESSIONS TEST

A 다음 영어는 한글로, 한글은 영어로 쓰시오.

1 play tennis	_____	**6** 사진을 찍다	_____
2 listen to music	_____	**7** 카메라	_____
3 free time	_____	**8** 취미	_____
4 play computer games	_____	**9** 영화를 보다	_____
5 read	_____	**10** 퍼즐을 맞추다	_____

B 다음 문장을 해석하시오.

1 That sounds good.

→ _____

2 I like to play computer games.

→ _____

3 What do you like to do in your free time?

→ _____

4 How about listening to music?

→ _____

WoW!

18

UNIT 8 AT THE FESTIVAL

WORDS

듣고 따라 말해 봅시다.

□ **sing** [siŋ]	노래하다	□ **watch the fireworks**	불꽃놀이를 보다
□ **dance on a stage**	무대 위에서 춤추다	□ **festival** [féstivəl]	축제
□ **look for a restroom**	화장실을 찾다	□ **join** [dʒɔin]	함께 하다
□ **eat snacks**	간식을 먹다	□ **a lot of**	많은
□ **drink soda**	탄산음료를 마시다	□ **people** [pí:pl]	사람들

EXPRESSIONS

듣고 따라 말해 봅시다.

□ A: What are they doing? (그들은 무엇을 하고 있는 거야?)
  B: They are dancing on the stage. (그들은 무대 위에서 춤추고 있어.)

□ A: Can I drink some soda? (탄산음료 좀 마셔도 돼요?)
  B: Yes, you can. / Sure. Go ahead. (그럼, 마시렴. / 물론이지. 그렇게 하렴.)

□ A: Can I help you? (도와줄까?)
  B: Yes, please. I'm looking for a restroom. (네. 전 화장실을 찾고 있어요.)

WORDS & EXPRESSIONS TEST

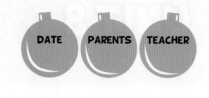

DATE   PARENTS   TEACHER

A 다음 영어는 한글로, 한글은 영어로 쓰시오.

1 sing   _____

2 drink soda   _____

3 eat snacks   _____

4 join   _____

5 a lot of   _____

6 사람들   _____

7 무대 위에서 춤추다   _____

8 축제   _____

9 불꽃놀이를 보다   _____

10 화장실을 찾다   _____

B 다음을 바르게 배열하여 문장을 완성하시오.

1 soda / drink / can / I / some / ?

   → _____

2 help / I / you / can / ?

   → _____

3 are / they / on / dancing / the stage / .

   → _____

4 they / doing / are / what / ?

   → _____

WoW!

20

UNIT 9 COOKING

WORDS

듣고 따라 말해 봅시다.

☐ **wash** [waʃ]	씻다	☐ **spicy** [spáisi]	매운
☐ **peel** [pi:l]	껍질을 벗기다	☐ **taste** [teist]	~한 맛이 나다
☐ **mix** [miks]	섞다	☐ **try** [trai]	먹어보다, 마셔 보다
☐ **fry** [frai]	튀기다	☐ **smell** [smel]	냄새가 나다
☐ **sweet** [swi:t]	달콤한	☐ **delicious** [dilíʃəs]	맛있는
☐ **salty** [sɔ́:lti]	짠	☐ **salt** [sɔ:lt]	소금
☐ **sour** [sauər]	신	☐ **sugar** [ʃúgər]	설탕

EXPRESSIONS

듣고 따라 말해 봅시다.

☐ A: Will you wash the tomatoes? (토마토 좀 씻어줄래?)
  B: Okay, I will. (응, 그럴게.)

☐ A: How does it taste? (그것은 맛이 어떠니?)
  B: It's very salty. (너무 짜.)

21

WORDS & EXPRESSIONS TEST

A 다음 영어는 한글로, 한글은 영어로 쓰시오.

1 peel _____

2 sugar _____

3 fry _____

4 try _____

5 taste _____

6 salty _____

7 매운 _____

8 달콤한 _____

9 맛있는 _____

10 섞다 _____

11 씻다 _____

12 소금 _____

B 다음 문장을 해석하시오.

1 How does it taste?

→ _____

2 Will you wash the tomatoes?

→ _____

3 It's very salty.

→ _____

UNIT 10 SHOPPING

WORDS

듣고 따라 말해 봅시다.

□ **shirt** [ʃəːrt]	셔츠	□ **umbrella** [ʌmbrélə]	우산
□ **jacket** [dʒǽkit]	재킷	□ **size** [saiz]	(옷 등의) 사이즈, 치수
□ **skirt** [skəːrt]	치마	□ **wear** [wɛər]	입다, 신다, 쓰다
□ **pants** [pænts]	바지	□ **try on**	~을 입어보다, 신어보다
□ **shoes** [ʃuːz]	구두	□ **medium** [míːdiəm]	중간의
□ **gloves** [glʌvz]	장갑	□ **large** [lɑːrdʒ]	큰

EXPRESSIONS

듣고 따라 말해 봅시다.

□ A: May I help you? (도와드릴까요?)
　 B: Yes. I'm looking for a shirt. (네. 저는 셔츠를 찾고 있어요.)

□ A: How much is this skirt? (이 치마 얼마예요?)
　 B: It's twelve dollars. (12달러입니다.)

□ A: What size do you wear? (사이즈가 어떻게 되세요?)
　 B: I wear a small. (작은 사이즈를 입어요.)

WORDS & EXPRESSIONS TEST

A 다음 영어는 한글로, 한글은 영어로 쓰시오.

1 shoes   _____

2 umbrella   _____

3 wear   _____

4 medium   _____

5 try on   _____

6 장갑 _____

7 바지 _____

8 재킷 _____

9 셔츠 _____

10 치마 _____

B 다음 우리말을 바르게 영작하시오.

1 저는 셔츠를 찾고 있어요.

→ _____ _____ _____ _____ .

2 이 치마 얼마예요?

→ _____ _____ _____ _____ ?

3 도와드릴까요?

→ _____ _____ _____ _____ ?

4 사이즈가 어떻게 되세요?

→ _____ _____ _____ _____ ?

WoW!

24

부록

★ NUMBERS

1	one
2	two
3	three
4	four
5	five
6	six
7	seven
8	eight
9	nine
10	ten
11	eleven
12	twelve
13	thirteen
14	fourteen
15	fifteen
16	sixteen

17	seventeen
18	eighteen
19	nineteen
20	twenty
21	twenty-one
22	twenty-two
23	twenty-three
24	twenty-four
30	thirty
40	forty
50	fifty
60	sixty
70	seventy
80	eighty
90	ninety
100	one hundred

★ FRUITS & VEGETABLES

apple

orange

strawberry

grape

peach

watermelon

tomato

potato

onion

cucumber

carrot

mushroom

WORDS & EXPRESSIONS TEST 정답

UNIT 1 COLORS AND SHAPES

P. 6

A 1 파란색의 2 삼각형 3 시계 4 원형
5 찾다, 발견하다 6 square 7 green
8 button 9 yellow 10 rectangle

B 1 그것은 무슨 모양이니?
2 빨간색이야.
3 원형이야.
4 그것은 무슨 색이니?

UNIT 2 EVERYDAY LIFE

P. 8

A 1 학교에 가다 2 일어나다 3 숙제를 하다
4 일찍 5 ~의 후에[뒤에] 6 have lunch
7 exercise 8 late 9 go to bed
10 go home

B 1 It's time to get up.
2 I go to bed at 12 o'clock.
3 What time do you go to bed?
4 What time is it?

UNIT 3 FEELINGS

P. 10

A 1 무서워하는 2 지루한 3 피곤한
4 밖에, 밖으로 5 아픈 6 excited
7 worried 8 angry 9 sad 10 noisy

B 1 Are, you, scared

2 How, do, you, feel
3 I'm, excited

UNIT 4 BODY PARTS

P. 12

A 1 다리 2 귀 3 발 4 입 5 큰 6 arm
7 leg 8 nose 9 small 10 short

B 1 그것은 어떻게 생겼니?
2 그것은 눈이 몇 개니?
3 그것은 귀가 커.
4 그것은 눈이 세 개야.

UNIT 5 AT HOME

P. 14

A 1 서랍 2 ~ 안에, ~ 속에 3 탁자 4 양말
5 열쇠 6 chair 7 watch 8 bookshelf
9 under 10 glasses

B 1 They are mine.
2 It's in the drawer.
3 Where is my car key?
4 Whose socks are these?

UNIT 6 SCHOOL SUBJECTS

P. 16

A 1 수학 2 미술 3 과학 4 어려운
5 ~에 관심이 있다 6 history 7 boring
8 favorite 9 English 10 music

Ⓑ 1 Are, you, interested, in, painting
2 My, favorite, subject, is, science
3 What's, your, favorite, subject
4 I, like, art, class

UNIT 7 HOBBIES

P. 18

Ⓐ 1 테니스를 치다   2 음악을 듣다   3 여가시간
4 컴퓨터 게임을 하다   5 (책 등을) 읽다
6 take photos   7 camera   8 hobby
9 watch movies   10 do puzzles

Ⓑ 1 좋은 생각이야.
2 나는 컴퓨터 게임 하는 것을 좋아해.
3 너는 여가시간에 무엇을 하는 것을 좋아하니?
4 음악 듣는 게 어때?

UNIT 8 AT THE FESTIVAL

P. 20

Ⓐ 1 노래하다   2 탄산음료를 마시다   3 간식을 먹다
4 함께 하다   5 많은   6 people
7 dance on a stage   8 festival
9 watch the fireworks
10 look for a restroom

Ⓑ 1 Can I drink some soda?
2 Can I help you?
3 They are dancing on the stage.
4 What are they doing?

UNIT 9 COOKING

P. 22

Ⓐ 1 껍질을 벗기다   2 설탕   3 튀기다
4 먹어보다, 마셔보다   5 ~한 맛이 나다   6 짠

7 spicy   8 sweet   9 delicious   10 mix
11 wash   12 salt

Ⓑ 1 그것은 맛이 어떠니?
2 토마토 좀 씻어줄래?
3 그것은 너무 짜.

UNIT 10 SHOPPING

P. 24

Ⓐ 1 구두   2 우산   3 입다, 신다, 쓰다   4 중간의
5 ~을 입어보다, 신어보다   6 gloves   7 pants
8 jacket   9 shirt   10 skirt

Ⓑ 1 I'm, looking, for, a, shirt
2 How, much, is, this, skirt
3 May, I, help, you
4 What, size, do, you, wear

초등학생의 영어 친구
리스닝버디
LISTENING BUDDY 2

Dear Friends,

I'm your English Buddy!
Forget about all your worries.
I'm here to help you!
Let's smile! Let's learn! And let's have fun!

All the best,
Your English Buddy

★ HOW TO USE ★

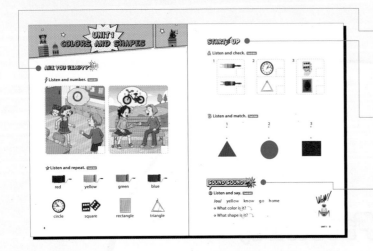

ARE YOU READY
그림을 보면서 본문에서 다룰 주요 단어와 표현을 학습합니다.

START UP
간단한 문제를 통해 학습한 단어와 표현을 확인합니다.

SOUND SOUND
주의해야 할 발음과 억양을 듣고 따라 함으로써 올바른 영어 발음을 익힐 수 있습니다.

LISTEN UP
반복적·단계적으로 구성된 대화를 듣고 연습 문제를 풀어봄으로써, 주요 의사소통 기능을 자연스럽게 습득할 수 있습니다.

LET'S SPEAK WITH BUDDY
재미있는 만화와 함께 배운 표현들을 복습합니다. 제시된 대체 어휘들을 이용하여 친구와 역할극을 해 봅니다.

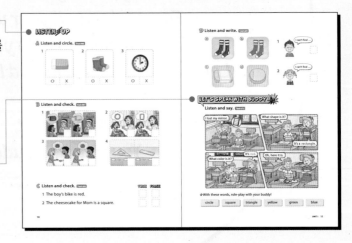

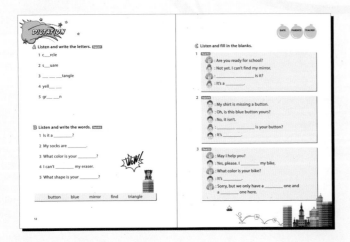

DICTATION
앞에서 학습한 내용을 다시 한 번 듣고 받아 써 봅니다. 단어, 문장, 대화 순으로 체계적인 받아쓰기 학습을 할 수 있습니다.

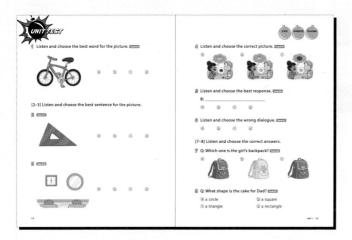

UNIT TEST

해당 Unit에서 배운 내용을 아우르는 다양한
유형의 실전 문제를 통해, 학습한 내용을 충실히
이해했는지 확인할 수 있습니다.

REVIEW TEST

3~4개의 Unit을 학습한 후, 총 10문항으로 구성
된 누적 테스트를 풀어봄으로써 앞서 배운 내용에
대한 성취도를 확인할 수 있습니다.

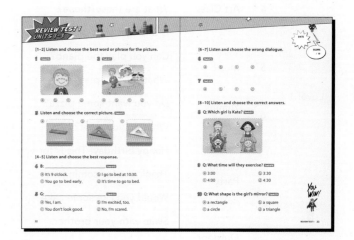

단어장

본책에서 학습한 단어와 표현이 보기 쉽게 정리되어 있습니다.
단어와 표현을 충분히 학습했는지 확인해 볼 수 있도록 간단한
테스트도 함께 제공됩니다.
단어와 표현에 대한 발음은 QR코드를 통해 손쉽게 확인 가능
합니다.

☆ OVERVIEW OF LISTENING BUDDY ☆

Level	Unit	Title	Key Expressions	Key Words
Level 1	1	Greetings	Good morning. How are you? What's your name? This is my friend, Brian.	morning, afternoon, evening, name, friend, meet, nice
	2	My Family	Who is he? How old is she?	grandfather, grandmother, father, mother, brother, sister, uncle, aunt, cousin, twins
	3	Pets	Do you like birds? Do you have any pets?	dog, cat, rabbit, hamster, bird, fish, turtle, lizard
	4	Art Class	What is this/that? What are these/those? Is this/that your glue?	crayon, colored pencil, eraser, sketchbook, glue, scissors, ruler
	5	Music	Can you play the piano? What can you play?	piano, violin, cello, flute, guitar, drums, trumpet
	6	Yummy Food	Do you want some pizza? What do you want?	bread, sandwich, salad, pizza, chicken, noodles, fried rice
	7	Birthday Party	Happy birthday! This is for you. Thank you for coming. Would you like some cake?	card, cake, present, hairpin, robot, backpack, hat
	8	Outdoor Activities	Swim with your brother. Don't ride your bike here. Watch out! / Be careful!	swim, ride, catch, throw, climb up, push, wear
	9	Seven Days	What day is it today? What do you do on Sundays?	Sunday, Monday, Tuesday, Wednesday, Thursday, Friday, Saturday, play soccer, go hiking, have a yoga class, visit my uncle
	10	Weather	How's the weather? / What's the weather like? Let's play soccer outside.	sunny, cloudy, windy, rainy, snowy, hot, cold
Level 2	1	Colors and Shapes	What color is it? What shape is it?	red, yellow, green, blue, circle, square, rectangle, triangle
	2	Everyday Life	What time is it? What time do you go to bed?	get up, go to school, have lunch, go home, exercise, do homework, go to bed
	3	Feelings	How do you feel? Are you scared?	happy, sad, excited, angry, scared, bored, worried, tired
	4	Body Parts	What does it look like? How many eyes does it have?	eye, nose, mouth, ear, arm, hand, leg, foot

Level	Unit	Title	Key Expressions	Key Words
Level 2	5	At Home	Where is my car key? Whose socks are these?	key, watch, socks, glasses, bed, table, drawer, bookshelf
	6	School Subjects	What's your favorite subject? Are you interested in painting?	art, music, English, math, science, P.E., history
	7	Hobbies	What do you like to do in your free time? How about playing tennis after school?	listen to music, play tennis, watch movies, take photos, play computer games, do puzzles
	8	At the Festival	What are they doing? Can I drink some soda?	sing, dance on a stage, look for a restroom, eat snacks, drink soda, watch the fireworks
	9	Cooking	Will you wash the tomatoes? How does it taste?	wash, peel, mix, fry, sweet, salty, sour, spicy
	10	Shopping	I'm looking for a shirt. How much is this skirt? What size do you wear?	shirt, jacket, skirt, pants, shoes, gloves, umbrella
Level 3	1	People Around Me	What does she look like? What is she like?	tall, short, thin, fat, shy, outgoing, funny, lazy
	2	Jobs	What does your father do? What do you want to be?	scientist, singer, police officer, firefighter, dentist, pilot, chef, vet
	3	Four Seasons	Which seasons do you like? Why do you like summer?	spring, summer, fall, winter, go on a picnic, play at the beach, see colorful leaves, go skiing
	4	Sickness	I have a headache. You should see a doctor.	headache, toothache, stomachache, fever, cough, runny nose, sore throat, see a doctor, take medicine
	5	At the Restaurant	Are you ready to order? What would you like to have? May I have the bill, please?	order, menu, bill, dessert, steak, hamburger, French fries, pie
	6	Special Days	What's the date today? When is your birthday?	January, February, March, April, May, June, July, August, September, October, November, December, New Year's Day, Earth Day, Halloween, Christmas
	7	The Past	What did you do yesterday? How was your weekend?	played baseball, watched TV, visited a museum, went swimming, had a party, took a trip
	8	Phone Calls	May I speak to Amy? Who's calling, please? May I leave a message?	answer the phone, hold on, leave a message, call back, hang up, have the wrong number
	9	My Town	Where is the bakery? How can I get to the movie theater? Go straight and turn left.	library, bank, hospital, bakery, movie theater, turn left, turn right, go straight, next to, between
	10	Plans	What are you going to do tomorrow? Do you have any plans for your vacation?	go shopping, get a haircut, relax at home, go camping, study Chinese, travel overseas

★ CONTENTS ★

Let's meet our buddies in Listening Buddy!

Ann   Tom   Jack   Jenny   Kevin

UNIT 1
COLORS AND SHAPES

ARE YOU READY?

⚡ Listen and number. `Track 001`

☆ Listen and repeat. `Track 002`

red

yellow

green

blue

circle

square

rectangle

triangle

A Listen and check. Track 003

1
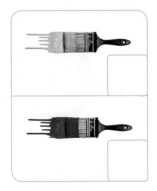

2
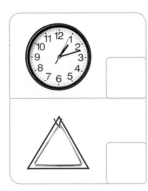

3

B Listen and match. Track 004

1
·

2
·

3
·

·

·

·

SOUND SOUND

◎ Listen and say. Track 005

/ou/ yellow know go home

• What color is it?

• What shape is it?

LISTEN UP

A Listen and circle. `Track 006`

1

O   X

2

O   X

3

O   X

B Listen and check. `Track 007`

1

2

3

4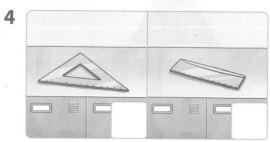

C Listen and check. `Track 008`

                                                                                       TRUE   FALSE

1 The boy's bike is red.

2 The cheesecake for Mom is a square.

10

⑩ Listen and write. Track 009

ⓐ

ⓑ

ⓒ

ⓓ

1  I can't find …

2  I can't find …

LET'S SPEAK WITH BUDDY

Listen and say. Track 010

➕ With these words, role-play with your buddy!

circle	square	triangle	yellow	green	blue

DICTATION

A Listen and write the letters. `Track 011`

1 c___rcle

2 s___uare

3 ___ ___ ___tangle

4 yell___ ___

5 gr___ ___n

B Listen and write the words. `Track 012`

1 Is it a _____?

2 My socks are _____.

3 What color is your _____?

4 I can't _____ my eraser.

5 What shape is your _____?

| button | blue | mirror | find | triangle |

DATE　PARENTS　TEACHER

☾ Listen and fill in the blanks.

1 `Track 013`

 : Are you ready for school?

 : Not yet. I can't find my mirror.

 : _____ _____ is it?

 : It's a _____ .

2 `Track 014`

 : My shirt is missing a button.

 : Oh, is this blue button yours?

 : No, it isn't.

 : _____ _____ is your button?

 : It's _____ .

3 `Track 015`

 : May I help you?

 : Yes, please. I _____ my bike.

 : What color is your bike?

 : It's _____ .

 : Sorry, but we only have a _____ one and
a _____ one here.

1 Listen and choose the best word for the picture. Track 016

ⓐ   ⓑ   ⓒ   ⓓ

[2-3] Listen and choose the best sentence for the picture.

2 Track 017

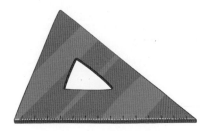

ⓐ   ⓑ   ⓒ   ⓓ

3 Track 018

ⓐ   ⓑ   ⓒ   ⓓ

4 Listen and choose the correct picture. Track 019

ⓐ  ⓑ  ⓒ

5 Listen and choose the best response. Track 020

B: _____

ⓐ   ⓑ   ⓒ   ⓓ

6 Listen and choose the wrong dialogue. Track 021

ⓐ   ⓑ   ⓒ   ⓓ

[7–8] Listen and choose the correct answers.

7 Q: Which one is the girl's backpack? Track 022

ⓐ  ⓑ  ⓒ

8 Q: What shape is the cake for Dad? Track 023

ⓐ a circle   ⓑ a square

ⓒ a triangle   ⓓ a rectangle

ARE YOU READY?

⚡ **Listen and number.** Track 024

☆ **Listen and repeat.** Track 025

get up

go to school

have lunch

go home

exercise

do homework

go to bed

A Listen and number. `Track 026`

☐ ☐ ☐ ☐

B Listen and match. `Track 027`

1   2   3
•   •   •

•   •   •

Listen and say. `Track 028`

/ʌ/   lunch   fun   month   love

○ What time is it? ↘

○ What time do you go to bed? ↘

LISTEN UP

A Listen and match. Track 029

1

2

3

•   •   •

•   •   •

B Listen and check. Track 030

1

2

3

4

C Listen and check. Track 031

TRUE   FALSE

1 The girl goes to bed at 9:30.

2 The children will have lunch at 12.

D Listen and number in time order. Track 032

LET'S SPEAK WITH BUDDY

Listen and say. Track 033

✛ Listen again and repeat.

DICTATION

A **Listen and write the words.** `Track 034`

1 _____ up

2 go _____

3 go to _____

4 have _____

5 go to _____

B **Listen and write the words.** `Track 035`

1 _____ time is it now?

2 I _____ at 5:30.

3 It's _____ to go to bed.

4 What time do you do your _____?

5 Let's _____ lunch after that.

| homework | time | have | what | exercise |

C Listen and fill in the blanks.

1 Track 036

: What time do you _____ _____ in the morning?

: I get up at 7 o'clock. How about you?

: I get up _____ _____ o'clock.

: Wow, you get up early.

2 Track 037

: What time do you go _____ _____?

: I go to bed at 11:30.

: Oh, that's _____ _____.

: How about you?

: I go to bed at 9:30.

3 Track 038

: _____ _____ is it now?

: It's 12 o'clock.

: Oh, it's time to _____ _____.

: I'm not hungry. Let's play one more game.

: Okay. Then let's have lunch _____ that.

: Sounds good!

UNIT 2 21

UNIT TEST

1 Listen and choose the best phrase for the picture. [Track 039]

ⓐ   ⓑ   ⓒ   ⓓ

2 Listen and choose the best sentence for the picture. [Track 040]

ⓐ   ⓑ   ⓒ   ⓓ

3 Listen and choose the correct picture. [Track 041]

ⓐ    ⓑ    ⓒ

4 Look, listen, and choose the answer. `Track 042`

ⓐ   ⓑ   ⓒ   ⓓ

5 Listen and choose the best response. `Track 043`

B: _____

ⓐ   ⓑ   ⓒ   ⓓ

6 Listen and choose the wrong dialogue. `Track 044`

ⓐ   ⓑ   ⓒ   ⓓ

[7–8] Listen and choose the correct answers.

7 Q: What will the boy and the girl do next? `Track 045`

ⓐ    ⓑ    ⓒ

8 Q: What time does the boy go to bed? `Track 046`

ⓐ 9:00   ⓑ 9:30   ⓒ 10:00   ⓓ 10:30

UNIT 3
FEELINGS

⚡ **Listen and number.** Track 047

☆ **Listen and repeat.** Track 048

happy

sad

excited

angry

scared

bored

worried

tired

START UP

A Listen and number. `Track 049`

B Listen and match. `Track 050`

1 •   2 •   3 •

•   •   •

SOUND SOUND

Listen and say. `Track 051`

/ɔː/   bored   short   more   score

• How do you feel? ↘

• Are you scared? ↗

LISTEN UP

A Listen and match. `Track 052`

1	2	3
Alex	Kate	Sam

• • •

• • •

| bored | angry | happy |

B Listen and check. `Track 053`

C Listen and check. `Track 054`

1 The boy feels tired.

2 The girl is worried about the test.

TRUE FALSE

26

1   Elly   ⓐ   ⓑ   ⓒ

2   Josh   ⓐ   ⓑ   ⓒ

LET'S SPEAK WITH BUDDY

Listen and say. Track 056

How do you feel today?

I'm happy. It's a beautiful day!

How about you?

I'm stressed.   Why?

All the girls like me.

✛ Listen again and repeat.

DICTATION

A **Listen and write the letters.** `Track 057`

1 t___red

2 b___red

3 ha___ ___y

4 ___ ___gry

5 ___ ___cited

B **Listen and write the words.** `Track 058`

1 How do you _____ today?

2 I'm so _____ .

3 I feel _____ .

4 Are you _____ ?

5 You _____ happy.

| worried | look | sad | feel | scared |

C Listen and fill in the blanks.

1 Track 059

: Alex, _____ do you feel?

: I'm so _____. It's noisy outside.
I can't sleep.

2 Track 060

: Are you okay? You don't look _____.

: Look over there! There's a spider.
I'm so _____.

: Don't _____. I'll take it outside.

: Thank you.

3 Track 061

 : How do you feel today?

 : I'm _____. How about you?

 : I feel _____.

 : Let's go out. It's a beautiful day!

 : Sorry, but I'm too _____.

UNIT TEST

1 Listen and choose the best word for the picture. `Track 062`

ⓐ   ⓑ   ⓒ   ⓓ

2 Listen and choose the best sentence for the picture. `Track 063`

ⓐ   ⓑ   ⓒ   ⓓ

3 Listen and choose the correct picture. `Track 064`

ⓐ    ⓑ    ⓒ

4 Look, listen, and choose the answer. `Track 065`

ⓐ   ⓑ   ⓒ   ⓓ

5 Listen and choose the best response. `Track 066`

B: _____

ⓐ   ⓑ   ⓒ   ⓓ

6 Listen and choose the wrong dialogue. `Track 067`

ⓐ   ⓑ   ⓒ   ⓓ

[7–8] Listen and choose the correct answers.

 Q: How does the girl feel? `Track 068`

ⓐ    ⓑ    ⓒ

8 Q: The boy feels _____ . `Track 069`

ⓐ happy   ⓑ sad

ⓒ tired   ⓓ scared

[1–2] Listen and choose the best word or phrase for the picture.

1 Track 070

ⓐ   ⓑ   ⓒ   ⓓ

2 Track 071

ⓐ   ⓑ   ⓒ   ⓓ

3 Listen and choose the correct picture. Track 072

ⓐ    ⓑ    ⓒ

[4–5] Listen and choose the best response.

4 B: _____ Track 073

  ⓐ It's 9 o'clock.   ⓑ I go to bed at 10:30.

  ⓒ You go to bed early.   ⓓ It's time to go to bed.

5 G: _____ Track 074

  ⓐ Yes, I am.   ⓑ I'm excited, too.

  ⓒ You don't look good.   ⓓ No, I'm scared.

[6–7] Listen and choose the wrong dialogue.

6 `Track 075`

ⓐ   ⓑ   ⓒ   ⓓ

7 `Track 076`

ⓐ   ⓑ   ⓒ   ⓓ

[8–10] Listen and choose the correct answers.

8 **Q: Which girl is Kate?** `Track 077`

9 **Q: What time will they exercise?** `Track 078`

ⓐ 3:00   ⓑ 3:30
ⓒ 4:00   ⓓ 4:30

10 **Q: What shape is the girl's mirror?** `Track 079`

ⓐ a rectangle   ⓑ a square
ⓒ a circle   ⓓ a triangle

UNIT 4
BODY PARTS

ARE YOU READY?

⚡ **Listen and number.** Track 080

☆ **Listen and repeat.** Track 081

eye

nose

mouth

ear

arm

hand

leg

foot

START UP

A Listen and number. Track 082

B Listen and match. Track 083

1   2   3

SOUND SOUND

Listen and say. Track 084

/z/   nose   size   rise   choose

o What does it look like?

o How many eyes does it have?

LISTEN UP

A Listen and number. `Track 085`

B Listen and check. `Track 086`

1

2

3

4
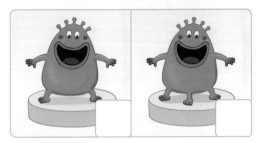

C Listen and check. `Track 087`

1 The boy's dog has long legs.

2 The monster has six short arms.

⒟ Listen and write. Track 088

ⓐ

ⓑ

ⓒ

ⓓ

1 Aki _____

2 Momo _____

LET'S SPEAK WITH BUDDY

Listen and say. Track 089

➕ Listen again and repeat.

DICTATION

A Listen and write the letters. `Track 090`

1 l___g

2 ___ ___ r

3 no___e

4 f___ ___t

5 mou___ ___

B Listen and write the words. `Track 091`

1 What does it _____ like?

2 It has short _____.

3 Does it have big _____?

4 How many _____ does it have?

5 It has three _____ feet.

| small | look | hands | arms | eyes |

38

C Listen and fill in the blanks.

1 `Track 092`

: Look at that! It looks strange.

: Yes, it does. It has a _____ _____.

: And it has a small _____.

: It looks funny.

2 `Track 093`

: The monster has many legs.

: _____ _____ legs does it have?

: It has _____ _____.

: Are you sure?

: Yes, I am.

3 `Track 094`

: Do you have any pets?

: Yes, I have a dog. He has big _____ and short legs. How about you?

: I have a dog, too.

: What does it _____ _____?

: She has small eyes and very big _____.

UNIT TEST

1 Listen and choose the best word for the picture. `Track 095`

ⓐ   ⓑ   ⓒ   ⓓ

2 Listen and choose the best sentence for the picture. `Track 096`

ⓐ   ⓑ   ⓒ   ⓓ

3 Listen and choose the correct picture. `Track 097`

ⓐ    ⓑ    ⓒ

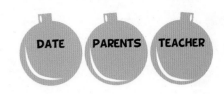
4 Look, listen, and choose the answer. Track 098

ⓐ　　　　ⓑ　　　　ⓒ　　　　ⓓ

5 Listen and choose the best response. Track 099

B: _____

ⓐ　　　ⓑ　　　ⓒ　　　ⓓ

6 Listen and choose the wrong dialogue. Track 100

ⓐ　　　ⓑ　　　ⓒ　　　ⓓ

[7–8] Listen and choose the correct answers.

7 Q: Which one is the boy's dog? Track 101

ⓐ 　　　ⓑ 　　　ⓒ

8 Q: How many arms does the monster have? Track 102

ⓐ one　　　　　　　ⓑ three

ⓒ five　　　　　　　ⓓ seven

UNIT 5
AT HOME

ARE YOU READY?

⚡ Listen and number. Track 103

☆ Listen and repeat. Track 104

key

watch

socks

glasses

bed

table

drawer

bookshelf

START UP

A Listen and number. Track 105

B Listen and match. Track 106

1 • 2 • 3 •

• • •

SOUND SOUND

Listen and say. Track 107

/k/ key   kind   class   /g/ glasses   glad   green

Listen and circle. Track 108

1 /k/   /g/   2 /k/   /g/   3 /k/   /g/

LISTEN UP

A Listen and match. Track 109

1   **2**   **3**

B Listen and check. Track 110

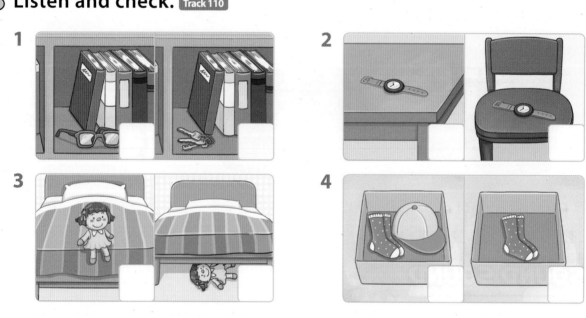

1   **2**

3   **4**

C Listen and check. Track 111

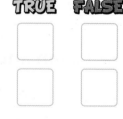

TRUE   FALSE

1 The key is on the bookshelf.

2 The socks under the bed are the boy's.

⒟ Listen and write. Track 112

1

2

LET'S SPEAK WITH BUDDY

Listen and say. Track 113

Where are my books?

Aren't they on the bookshelf?

No. Where are they?

Whose books are those? They're under the table.

Oh, those are my books!

✚ Listen again and repeat.

DICTATION

A **Listen and write the letters.** `Track 114`

1 ___ey

2 dr___ ___er

3 wat___ ___

4 so___ ___s

5 booksh___ ___f

B **Listen and write the words.** `Track 115`

1 _____ is my doll?

2 Whose _____ are these?

3 The ball is under the _____.

4 _____ cap is this?

5 The books are _____ the table.

| on | bed | whose | glasses | where |

⌒ Listen and fill in the blanks.

1 Track 116

 : _____ is my watch?

 : Whose _____ is that? It's _____ the bed.

 : Oh, that is my watch. Thank you, Dad.

 : Sure.

2 Track 117

 : Where is my car _____?

 : Isn't it on the _____?

 : No, it isn't there.

 : Then, how about _____ the drawer?

 : There it is! Thank you for your help.

3 Track 118

 : I can't see well. Where are my _____?

 : Whose glasses are those? They're on the _____.

 : Oh, those aren't _____. They're Dad's glasses.

 : Then, how about _____ the bookshelf?

 : Oh, there they are! Thank you, Mom.

UNIT TEST

1 Listen and choose the best word for the picture. Track 119

ⓐ   ⓑ   ⓒ   ⓓ

2 Listen and choose the best sentence for the picture. Track 120

ⓐ   ⓑ   ⓒ   ⓓ

3 Listen and choose the correct picture. Track 121

ⓐ    ⓑ    ⓒ

48

[4–5] Listen and choose the best response.

4 M: _____ Track 122

    ⓐ   ⓑ   ⓒ   ⓓ

5 G: _____ Track 123

    ⓐ   ⓑ   ⓒ   ⓓ

6 Listen and choose the wrong dialogue. Track 124

    ⓐ   ⓑ   ⓒ   ⓓ

[7–8] Listen and choose the correct answers.

7 Q: Where are the boy's socks? Track 125

ⓐ   ⓑ   ⓒ

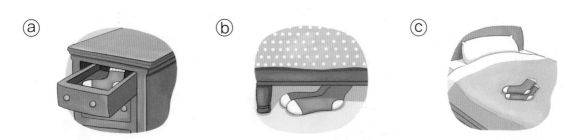

8 Q: What is on the bookshelf? Track 126

   ⓐ the girl's key   ⓑ the girl's box

   ⓒ Dad's car key   ⓓ the boy's box

UNIT 6
SCHOOL SUBJECTS

ARE YOU READY?

⚡ **Listen and number.** Track 127

☆ **Listen and repeat.** Track 128

art

music

English

math

science

P.E.

history

50

A Listen and number. Track 129

☐ ☐ ☐ ☐

B Listen and match. Track 130

1	2	3
Eric	Amy	Peter
•	•	•
•	•	•
music	history	English

SOUND SOUND

Listen and say. Track 131

Silent C science scissors scene muscle

○ What's your favorite subject? ↘

○ Are you interested in painting? ↗

WoW!

LISTEN UP

A Listen and circle. `Track 132`

1
😊 ☹️

2
😊 ☹️

3
😊 ☹️

B Listen and check. `Track 133`

1

2

3

4

C Listen and check. `Track 134`

TRUE   FALSE

1 The girl doesn't like science class.

☐ ☐

2 The boy's favorite subject is history.

☐ ☐

D Listen and write. Track 135

	MON	TUE	WED	THU	FRI
1		ⓑ ♪ #			
2	ⓐ + ÷			ⓓ 🧪	
3			ⓒ ⚽		ⓔ 🎨

Name	Favorite Subject
1 Sue	
2 Joe	
3 Ann	

LET'S SPEAK WITH BUDDY

Listen and say. Track 136

☘ Listen again and repeat.

DICTATION

A Listen and write the letters. `Track 137`

1 ___rt

2 ma___ ___

3 m___s___c

4 ___ ___ience

5 h___st___ry

B Listen and write the words. `Track 138`

1 What's your favorite _____?

2 Don't you _____ P.E.?

3 Are you _____ at art?

4 My favorite subject is _____.

5 Are you _____ in painting?

| good | like | interested | subject | English |

C Listen and fill in the blanks.

1 Track 139

 : Oh, no! We have _____ class today.

 : Don't you _____ music, Sue?

 : No, I don't. I like _____. It's my favorite subject.

2 Track 140

 : What's your _____ subject?

 : My favorite subject is _____.

 : Oh, really? Isn't it hard?

 : No, it's _____.

3 Track 141

 : What's your favorite subject?

 : My favorite subject is _____. How about you?

 : My favorite subject is _____.

 : Oh, really?

 : Yes. _____ you like history?

 : No, I don't. I'm not _____ in it.

UNIT TEST

1 Listen and choose the best word for the picture. Track 142

ⓐ   ⓑ   ⓒ   ⓓ

2 Listen and choose the best sentence for the picture. Track 143

ⓐ   ⓑ   ⓒ   ⓓ

3 Listen and choose the correct picture. Track 144

ⓐ    ⓑ    ⓒ

4 Listen and choose the best dialogue for the picture. Track 145

ⓐ   ⓑ   ⓒ   ⓓ

5 Listen and choose the best response. Track 146

B: _____

ⓐ   ⓑ   ⓒ   ⓓ

6 Listen and choose the wrong dialogue. Track 147

ⓐ   ⓑ   ⓒ   ⓓ

[7–8] Listen and choose the correct answers.

7 Q: What is the boy's favorite subject? Track 148

ⓐ    ⓑ    ⓒ

8 Q: The girl is interested in _____. Track 149

ⓐ art   ⓑ P.E.

ⓒ English   ⓓ history

[1–2] Listen and choose the best word for the picture.

1 `Track 150`

ⓐ   ⓑ   ⓒ   ⓓ

2 `Track 151`

ⓐ   ⓑ   ⓒ   ⓓ

3 Listen and choose the correct picture. `Track 152`

ⓐ    ⓑ    ⓒ

[4–5] Listen and choose the best response.

4 B: _____ `Track 153`

   ⓐ They're not mine.   ⓑ It's on the table.

   ⓒ That is my key.   ⓓ It isn't there.

5 G: _____ `Track 154`

   ⓐ No, it's fun.   ⓑ Yes, I'm interested in art.

   ⓒ No, I'm not good at P.E.   ⓓ Yes, it's my favorite subject.

[6–7] Listen and choose the wrong dialogue.

6 `Track 155`

ⓐ   ⓑ   ⓒ   ⓓ

7 `Track 156`

ⓐ   ⓑ   ⓒ   ⓓ

[8–10] Listen and choose the correct answers.

8 Q: Where are the girl's glasses? `Track 157`

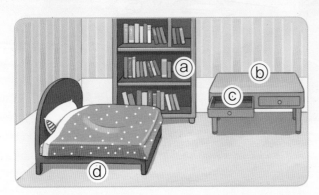

9 Q: Pepi has big _____ and short _____. `Track 158`

ⓐ eyes, legs   ⓑ eyes, arms

ⓒ ears, legs   ⓓ ears, arms

10 Q: The boy's favorite subject is _____. `Track 159`

ⓐ music   ⓑ math

ⓒ art   ⓓ history

UNIT 7 HOBBIES

ARE YOU READY?

⚡ Listen and number. Track 160

☆ Listen and repeat. Track 161

listen to music

play tennis

watch movies

take photos

play computer games

do puzzles

START UP

A Listen and number. Track 162

B Listen and match. Track 163

1   2   3

SOUND SOUND

Listen and say. Track 164

Silent T   listen   Christmas   castle

- What do you like to do in your free time?
- How about playing tennis after school?

WoW!

LISTEN UP

A Listen and circle. Track 165

1

2

3

B Listen and check. Track 166

1

2

3

4

C Listen and check. Track 167

	TRUE	FALSE
1 They will do puzzles after school.	☐	☐
2 The girl likes to take photos.	☐	☐

Ⓓ **Listen and mark.** Track 168

1 I like to …					
2 I like to …					
3 I like to …					

LET'S SPEAK WITH BUDDY

Listen and say. Track 169

Do you like to go swimming?

No, I don't. I can't swim.

What do you like to do?

I like to go swimming.

Oh, I like to go swimming, too! It's my favorite hobby.

Let's go swimming!

✛Listen again and repeat.

DICTATION

A **Listen and write the words.** Track 170

1 play _____

2 take _____

3 _____ movies

4 _____ to music

5 play computer _____

B **Listen and write the words.** Track 171

1 What do you like to _____ in your free time?

2 I like to _____ books.

3 How about doing _____ after school?

4 Does she like to _____ photos?

5 I like to go _____ with my father.

| take | do | read | swimming | puzzles |

ℂ Listen and fill in the blanks.

1 `Track 172`

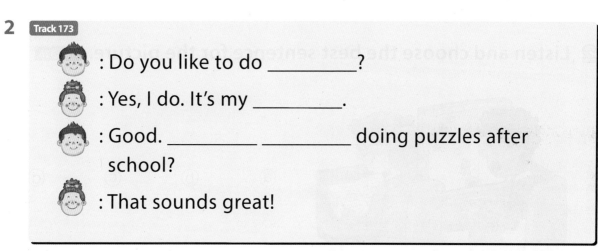

: David, what do you _____ to do in your free time?

: I like to _____ sports.

: Do you like to play _____?

: Yes, I do.

2 `Track 173`

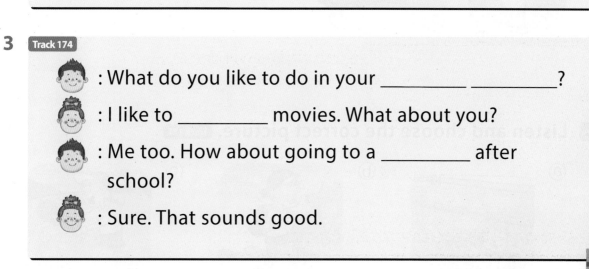

: Do you like to do _____?

: Yes, I do. It's my _____.

: Good. _____ _____ doing puzzles after school?

: That sounds great!

3 `Track 174`

: What do you like to do in your _____ _____?

: I like to _____ movies. What about you?

: Me too. How about going to a _____ after school?

: Sure. That sounds good.

UNIT TEST

1 **Listen and choose the best phrase for the picture.** Track 175

ⓐ   ⓑ   ⓒ   ⓓ

2 **Listen and choose the best sentence for the picture.** Track 176

ⓐ   ⓑ   ⓒ   ⓓ

3 **Listen and choose the correct picture.** Track 177

ⓐ    ⓑ    ⓒ

4 Listen and choose the best dialogue for the picture. `Track 178`

ⓐ   ⓑ   ⓒ   ⓓ

5 Listen and choose the best response. `Track 179`

G: _____

ⓐ   ⓑ   ⓒ   ⓓ

6 Listen and choose the wrong dialogue. `Track 180`

ⓐ   ⓑ   ⓒ   ⓓ

[7–8] Listen and choose the correct answers.

7 Q: What will they do? `Track 181`

ⓐ    ⓑ    ⓒ

8 Q: The girl likes to _____. `Track 182`

ⓐ play tennis   ⓑ read books

ⓒ watch movies   ⓓ take photos

UNIT 8
AT THE FESTIVAL

⚡ **Listen and number.** Track 183

☆ **Listen and repeat.** Track 184

sing

dance on a stage

look for a restroom

eat snacks

drink soda

watch the fireworks

68

START UP

A Listen and number. `Track 185`

B Listen and match. `Track 186`

1   2   3

SOUND SOUND

Listen and say. `Track 187`

/ŋ/ sing boring evening   /ŋk/ drink pink think

Listen and circle. `Track 188`

1 /ŋ/ /ŋk/   2 /ŋ/ /ŋk/   3 /ŋ/ /ŋk/

LISTEN UP

A Listen and number. `Track 189`

B Listen and check. `Track 190`

1

2

3

4

C Listen and check. `Track 191`

TRUE FALSE

1 The boy is singing in front of people.

2 The girl will take a photo.

D Listen and write. `Track 192`

Find the people.

1 Ben _____

2 Lily _____

3 Mike _____

LET'S SPEAK WITH BUDDY

Listen and say. `Track 193`

✚ Listen again and repeat.

DICTATION

A **Listen and write the words.** `Track 194`

    1 eat _____

    2 _____ soda

    3 dance on a _____

    4 _____ the fireworks

    5 look for a _____

B **Listen and write the words.** `Track 195`

    1 What are they _____?

    2 Are you _____ snacks?

    3 He is drinking _____.

    4 _____ I take a photo?

    5 She is _____ very well.

| eating | doing | can | singing | soda |

C Listen and fill in the blanks.

1 Track 196

 : What is she _____?

 : She is watching the _____.

 : Cool! Let's join her.

2 Track 197

 : Can I help you?

 : Yes, please. I'm _____ _____ a restroom.

 : There is a _____ over there.

3 Track 198

 : Dad, this festival is a lot of _____.

 : Yeah, it's _____!

 : Look over there. Is he _____ on the stage?

 : Yes, he is.

 : Can I take a _____?

 : Sure. Go ahead.

UNIT TEST

1 Listen and choose the best phrase for the picture. Track 199

ⓐ   ⓑ   ⓒ   ⓓ

2 Listen and choose the best sentence for the picture. Track 200

ⓐ   ⓑ   ⓒ   ⓓ

3 Listen and choose the correct picture. Track 201

ⓐ    ⓑ    ⓒ

4 Listen and choose the best dialogue for the picture. Track 202

ⓐ   ⓑ   ⓒ   ⓓ

5 Listen and choose the best response. Track 203

B: _____

ⓐ   ⓑ   ⓒ   ⓓ

6 Listen and choose the wrong dialogue. Track 204

ⓐ   ⓑ   ⓒ   ⓓ

[7–8] Listen and choose the correct answers.

7 Q: What is the girl doing? Track 205

ⓐ    ⓑ    ⓒ

8 Q: Who is singing on the stage? Track 206

ⓐ the boy   ⓑ the girl
ⓒ the boy's sister   ⓓ the girl's sister

UNIT 9 COOKING

ARE YOU READY?

⚡ **Listen and number.** Track 207

☆ **Listen and repeat.** Track 208

wash

peel

mix

fry

sweet

salty

sour

spicy

START UP

A Listen and number. Track 209

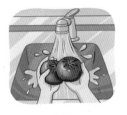

B Listen and match. Track 210

1
2
3

SOUND SOUND

Listen and say. Track 211

/iː/ peel sweet green meet

○ Will you wash the tomatoes? ↗

○ How does it taste? ↗

LISTEN UP

A Listen and match. Track 212

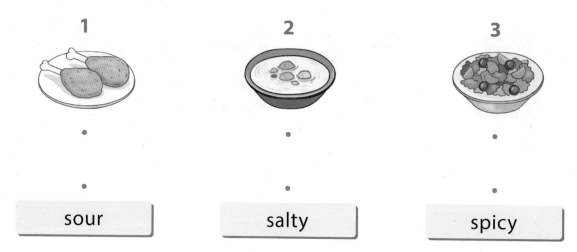

1	2	3

sour   salty   spicy

B Listen and check. Track 213

1

2

3

4

C Listen and check. Track 214

                                                        TRUE   FALSE

1 The girl will wash and fry the potatoes.

2 The lemonade tastes sour.

Ⓓ **Listen and number in order.** Track 215

LET'S SPEAK WITH BUDDY

Listen and say. Track 216

♦ Listen again and repeat.

DICTATION

A Listen and write the letters. Track 217

1 mi___

2 s___ ___r

3 sp___cy

4 wa___ ___

5 sw___ ___t

B Listen and write the words. Track 218

1 The chicken is _____.

2 Will you _____ the onions, please?

3 How does it _____?

4 Can I _____ this soup?

5 The lemonade tastes too _____.

| taste | try | fry | sour | salty |

C Listen and fill in the blanks.

1 Track 219

 : Do you want to _____ the soup?

 : Yes.

 : _____ does it taste?

 : It's _____.

2 Track 220

 : You look busy. What are you doing?

 : I'm _____ dinner.

 : Oh, I'll help you.

 : Thank you. _____ you _____ the salad, please?

 : Sure.

3 Track 221

 : Dad, are you making lunch?

 : Yes. I'm making _____. Can you _____ me?

 : Sure. What should I do?

 : Will you _____ and _____ the potatoes?

: Okay.

UNIT TEST

1 Listen and choose the best word for the picture. `Track 222`

ⓐ   ⓑ   ⓒ   ⓓ

2 Listen and choose the best sentence for the picture. `Track 223`

ⓐ   ⓑ   ⓒ   ⓓ

3 Listen and choose the correct picture. `Track 224`

ⓐ    ⓑ    ⓒ

4 **Look, listen, and choose the answer.** Track 225

ⓐ   ⓑ   ⓒ   ⓓ

5 **Listen and choose the best response.** Track 226

G: _____

ⓐ   ⓑ   ⓒ   ⓓ

6 **Listen and choose the wrong dialogue.** Track 227

ⓐ   ⓑ   ⓒ   ⓓ

[7–8] Listen and choose the correct answers.

7 **Q: What will the man do next?** Track 228

ⓐ    ⓑ    ⓒ

8 **Q: How does the soup taste?** Track 229

ⓐ sweet   ⓑ salty

ⓒ spicy   ⓓ sour

UNIT 10
SHOPPING

⚡ **Listen and number.** Track 230

☆ **Listen and repeat.** Track 231

shirt   jacket   skirt   pants

shoes   gloves   umbrella

84

START UP

A Listen and check. Track 232

1

2

3

B Listen and match. Track 233

1
•

2
•

3
•

•

•

•

SOUND SOUND

Listen and say. Track 234

/dʒ/   jacket   juice   jump   job

◦ How much is this skirt? ↘

◦ What size do you wear? ↘

WoW!

LISTEN UP

A Listen and match. `Track 235`

1 • •   • •  $5

2 • •  • • $6

3 • • • • $15

B Listen and check. `Track 236`

1

2

3

4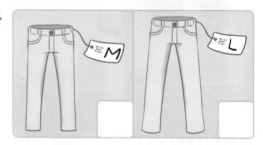

C Listen and check. `Track 237`

TRUE FALSE

1 The skirt is eight dollars. ☐ ☐

2 The boy will try on a blue jacket. ☐ ☐

D Listen and write. Track 238

LET'S SPEAK WITH BUDDY

Listen and say. Track 239

✦Listen again and repeat.

DICTATION

A **Listen and write the letters.** `Track 240`

1 sk___rt

2 glo___es

3 sh___ ___s

4 ___ ___cket

5 umb___ ___lla

B **Listen and write the words.** `Track 241`

1 I like it. I'll _____ it.

2 Can I _____ it on?

3 I'm looking for a _____.

4 What size do you _____?

5 How much are these _____?

| shirt | pants | wear | try | take |

C Listen and fill in the blanks.

1 Track 242

 : May I _____ you?

 : Yes, please. How much are these _____?

 : They are five dollars.

2 Track 243

 : Excuse me. _____ _____ is this shirt?

 : It's eight dollars.

 : Good. I'll _____ _____.

 : What _____ do you wear?

 : I wear a small.

3 Track 244

 : May I help you?

 : Yes, please. I'm looking for a _____.

 : What about this _____ jacket?

 : I like it. Can I _____ it _____?

 : Sure. What size do you wear?

 : I wear a medium.

UNIT TEST

1 **Listen and choose the best word for the picture.** Track 245

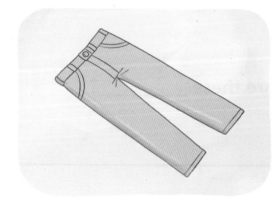

ⓐ   ⓑ   ⓒ   ⓓ

2 **Listen and choose the best sentence for the picture.** Track 246

ⓐ   ⓑ   ⓒ   ⓓ

3 **Listen and choose the correct picture.** Track 247

ⓐ    ⓑ    ⓒ

4 **Listen and choose the best dialogue for the picture.** `Track 248`

ⓐ   ⓑ   ⓒ   ⓓ

5 **Listen and choose the best response.** `Track 249`

M: _____

ⓐ   ⓑ   ⓒ   ⓓ

6 **Listen and choose the wrong dialogue.** `Track 250`

ⓐ   ⓑ   ⓒ   ⓓ

[7–8] Listen and choose the correct answers.

7 **Q: Which one will the boy buy?** `Track 251`

ⓐ    ⓑ    ⓒ

8 **Q: How much is the skirt?** `Track 252`

ⓐ $7   ⓑ $8   ⓒ $15   ⓓ $17

REVIEW TEST 3
UNITS 7~10

[1-2] Listen and choose the best word or phrase for the picture.

1 `Track 253`

ⓐ   ⓑ   ⓒ   ⓓ

2 `Track 254`

ⓐ   ⓑ   ⓒ   ⓓ

3 Listen and choose the correct picture. `Track 255`

ⓐ    ⓑ    ⓒ

[4-5] Listen and choose the best response.

4 B: _____ `Track 256`

  ⓐ It's ten dollars.   ⓑ What size do you wear?

  ⓒ I wear a small.   ⓓ I like it. Can I try it on?

5 G: _____ `Track 257`

  ⓐ She's singing.   ⓑ They are dancing very well.

  ⓒ Can I take a photo?   ⓓ I'm looking for her.

[6–7] Listen and choose the wrong dialogue.

6 Track 258

ⓐ   ⓑ   ⓒ   ⓓ

7 Track 259

ⓐ   ⓑ   ⓒ   ⓓ

[8–10] Listen and choose the correct answers.

8 Q: Which one will the girl buy? Track 260

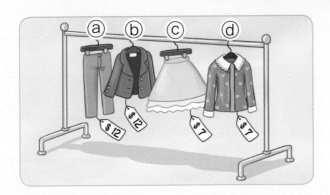

9 Q: The soup is _____ and the salad is _____. Track 261

ⓐ spicy, sweet   ⓑ salty, sour

ⓒ salty, sweet   ⓓ spicy, sour

10 Q: What does the girl's brother like to do? Track 262

ⓐ He likes to play tennis.   ⓑ He likes to listen to music.

ⓒ He likes to watch movies.   ⓓ He likes to play computer games.

지은이

NE능률 영어교육연구소

NE능률 영어교육연구소는 혁신적이며 효율적인 영어 교재를 개발하고
영어 학습의 질을 한 단계 높이고자 노력하는 NE능률의 연구조직입니다.

리스닝버디 2

펴 낸 이   주민홍
펴 낸 곳   서울특별시 마포구 월드컵북로 396(상암동) 누리꿈스퀘어 비즈니스타워 10층
            (주)NE능률 (우편번호 03925)
펴 낸 날   2016년 1월 5일 개정판 제1쇄
            2022년 11월 15일 제10쇄
전   화   02 2014 7114
팩   스   02 3142 0356
홈 페 이 지   www.neungyule.com
등 록 번 호   제 1-68호
I S B N   979-11-253-0973-4 63740
정   가   13,000원

NE 능률

고객센터

교재 내용 문의 : contact.nebooks.co.kr (별도의 가입 절차 없이 작성 가능)
제품 구매, 교환, 불량, 반품 문의 : 02-2014-7114
☎ 전화문의는 본사 업무시간 중에만 가능합니다.

NE능률 교재 MAP

아래 교재 MAP을 참고하여 본인의 현재 혹은 목표 수준에 따라 교재를 선택하세요.
NE능률 교재들과 함께 영어실력을 쑥쑥~ 올려보세요!
MP3 등 교재 부가 학습 서비스 및 자세한 교재 정보는 www.nebooks.co.kr 에서 확인하세요.

듣기
말하기
쓰기

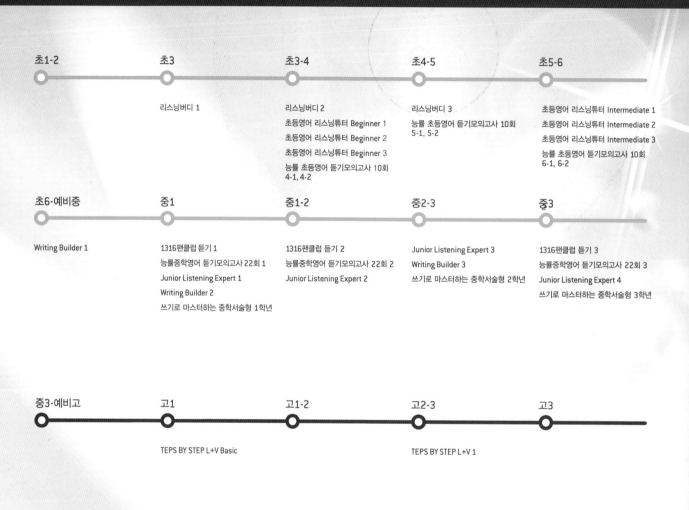

초1-2

초3
리스닝버디 1

초3-4
리스닝버디 2
초등영어 리스닝튜터 Beginner 1
초등영어 리스닝튜터 Beginner 2
초등영어 리스닝튜터 Beginner 3
능률 초등영어 듣기모의고사 10회
4-1, 4-2

초4-5
리스닝버디 3
능률 초등영어 듣기모의고사 10회
5-1, 5-2

초5-6
초등영어 리스닝튜터 Intermediate 1
초등영어 리스닝튜터 Intermediate 2
초등영어 리스닝튜터 Intermediate 3
능률 초등영어 듣기모의고사 10회
6-1, 6-2

초6-예비중
Writing Builder 1

중1
1316팬클럽 듣기 1
능률중학영어 듣기모의고사 22회 1
Junior Listening Expert 1
Writing Builder 2
쓰기로 마스터하는 중학서술형 1학년

중1-2
1316팬클럽 듣기 2
능률중학영어 듣기모의고사 22회 2
Junior Listening Expert 2

중2-3
Junior Listening Expert 3
Writing Builder 3
쓰기로 마스터하는 중학서술형 2학년

중3
1316팬클럽 듣기 3
능률중학영어 듣기모의고사 22회 3
Junior Listening Expert 4
쓰기로 마스터하는 중학서술형 3학년

중3-예비고

고1
TEPS BY STEP L+V Basic

고1-2

고2-3
TEPS BY STEP L+V 1

고3

수능 이상/
토플 80-89·
텝스 327-384점

수능 이상/
토플 90-99·
텝스 385-451점

수능 이상/
토플 100·
텝스 452점 이상

TEPS BY STEP L+V 2
RADIX TOEFL Blue Label Listening 1
RADIX TOEFL Blue Label Listening 2

RADIX TOEFL Black Label Listening 1

TEPS BY STEP L+V 3
RADIX TOEFL Black Label Listening 2

초등학생의 영어 친구

리스닝 버디

정답 및 해석

2

NE 능률

초등학생의 영어 친구

리스닝 버디

정답 및 해석

2

UNIT 1 COLORS AND SHAPES

ANSWERS

P.8

P.10

P.9

P.11

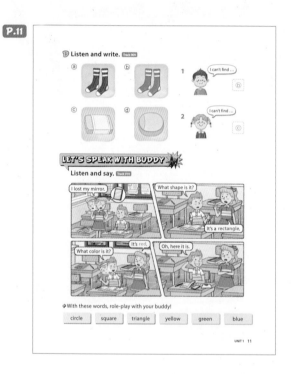

P.12~13 DICTATION

A 1 i   2 q   3 r, e, c
   4 o, w   5 e, e

B 1 triangle   2 blue   3 button
   4 find   5 mirror

C 1 What, shape, rectangle
     2 What, color, green
     3 lost, blue, red, yellow

P.14~15 **UNIT TEST**

1 ⓑ 2 ⓒ 3 ⓓ 4 ⓒ
5 ⓒ 6 ⓑ 7 ⓐ 8 ⓐ

SCRIPTS & 해석

P.8 **ARE YOU READY?**

⚡ **Listen and number.**

1 **G**: I have a new bike. (나는 새 자전거가 있어.)
  B: What color is it? (그것은 무슨 색이니?)
  G: It's red. (빨간색이야.)

2 **G**: I can't find my mirror. (거울을 못 찾겠어.)
  B: What shape is it? (그것은 무슨 모양이니?)
  G: It's a circle. (원형이야.)

⭐ **Listen and repeat.**

red (빨간색의)   yellow (노란색의)
green (초록색의)   blue (파란색의)
circle (원형)   square (정사각형)
rectangle (직사각형)   triangle (삼각형)

P.9 **START UP**

A **Listen and check.**

1 yellow (노란색의)
2 triangle (삼각형)
3 square (정사각형)

B **Listen and match.**

1 **G**: What color is it? (그것은 무슨 색이니?)
  B: It's green. (초록색이야.)

2 **G**: What shape is it? (그것은 무슨 모양이니?)
  B: It's a rectangle. (직사각형이야.)

3 **G**: What color is it? (그것은 무슨 색이니?)
  B: It's blue. (파란색이야.)

P.9 **SOUND SOUND**

🔵 **Listen and say.**

/ou/ yellow (노란색의)   know (알다)
     go (가다)   home (집)
○ What color is it? (그것은 무슨 색이니?)
○ What shape is it? (그것은 무슨 모양이니?)

P.10~11 **LISTEN UP**

A **Listen and circle.**

1 **G**: I can't find my eraser. (지우개를 못 찾겠어.)
  B: What shape is it? (그것은 무슨 모양이니?)
  G: It's a square. (정사각형이야.)

2 **B**: Mom, I can't find my socks.
      (엄마, 양말을 못 찾겠어요.)
  W: What color are they? (그것은 무슨 색이니?)
  B: They're blue. (파란색이에요.)

3 **G**: There's a new clock in our classroom.
      (교실에 새 시계가 있어.)
  B: What shape is it? (그것은 무슨 모양이니?)
  G: It's a circle. (원형이야.)

B **Listen and check.**

1 **B**: Can you help me, please? I lost my bag.
      (도와주시겠어요? 저는 가방을 잃어버렸어요.)
  M: What color is it? (그것은 무슨 색이니?)
  B: It's red. (빨간색이에요.)

2 **W**: Are you ready for school? (학교 갈 준비됐니?)
  G: Not yet. I can't find my mirror.
      (아직이요. 거울을 못 찾겠어요.)
  W: What shape is it? (그것은 무슨 모양이니?)
  G: It's a rectangle. (직사각형이에요.)

3 **B**: My shirt is missing a button.
      (셔츠 단추 하나가 없어졌어.)
  G: Oh, is this blue button yours?
      (오, 이 파란색 단추 네 거니?)
  B: No, it isn't. (아니, 그렇지 않아.)
  G: What color is your button?
      (네 단추는 무슨 색이니?)
  B: It's green. (초록색이야.)

4 **B**: There's a ruler over there. Is it yours?
      (저기 자가 하나 있는데. 저거 네 거니?)
  G: What color is the ruler? (그 자는 무슨 색이니?)
  B: It's yellow. (노란색이야.)
  G: Is it a triangle? (그것은 삼각형이니?)

B: Yes, it is. (응, 그래.)

C Listen and check.

1 W: May I help you? (도와드릴까요?)
   B: Yes, please. I lost my bike.
      (네. 저는 자전거를 잃어버렸어요.)
   W: What color is your bike?
      (당신의 자전거는 무슨 색인가요?)
   B: It's blue. (파란색이에요.)
   W: Sorry, but we only have a red one and a
      green one here.
      (죄송하지만, 여기에는 빨간색과 초록색 자전거만 있
      어요.)
   Question: The boy's bike is red.
             (소년의 자전거는 빨간색이다.)

2 B: Are you ready for Mom's birthday party?
      (엄마 생신 파티 준비됐니?)
   G: Yes, I have a cheesecake. Mom likes
      cheesecake.
      (응, 치즈케이크가 있어. 엄마는 치즈케이크를 좋아
      하셔.)
   B: Great! What shape is it?
      (잘했어! 그것은 무슨 모양이니?)
   G: It's a square. (정사각형이야.)
   Question: The cheesecake for Mom is a
             square.
             (엄마를 위한 치즈케이크는 정사각형이다.)

D Listen and write.

1 W: Are you ready for school? (학교 갈 준비됐니?)
   B: Not yet. I can't find my baseball socks.
      (아직이요. 야구 양말을 못 찾겠어요.)
   W: What color are they? (그것은 무슨 색이니?)
   B: They are green. (초록색이에요.)
   W: Here they are. (여기 있구나.)
   B: Thanks, Mom. (고마워요, 엄마.)

2 G: I can't find my eraser. It's yellow.
      (지우개를 못 찾겠어. 노란색이야.)
   B: Is this yours? (이거 네 거니?)
   G: No, it's not. (아니, 그렇지 않아.)
   B: What shape is it? (그것은 무슨 모양이니?)
   G: It's a rectangle. (직사각형이야.)

P.11 LET'S SPEAK WITH BUDDY

Listen and say.

Ann: I lost my mirror. (나 거울을 잃어버렸어.)

Jack: What shape is it? (그것은 무슨 모양이니?)
Ann: It's a rectangle. (직사각형이야.)

Jack: What color is it? (그것은 무슨 색이니?)
Ann: It's red. (빨간색이야.)

Jack: Oh, here it is. (오, 여기 있네.)

P.12~13 DICTATION

A 1 circle (원형)
  2 square (정사각형)
  3 rectangle (직사각형)
  4 yellow (노란색의)
  5 green (초록색의)

B 1 Is it a triangle? (그것은 삼각형이니?)
  2 My socks are blue. (내 양말은 파란색이야.)
  3 What color is your button?
    (네 단추는 무슨 색이니?)
  4 I can't find my eraser. (지우개를 못 찾겠어.)
  5 What shape is your mirror?
    (네 거울은 무슨 모양이니?)

C 1 W: Are you ready for school? (학교 갈 준비됐니?)
    G: Not yet. I can't find my mirror.
       (아직이요. 거울을 못 찾겠어요.)
    W: What shape is it? (그것은 무슨 모양이니?)
    G: It's a rectangle. (직사각형이에요.)

  2 B: My shirt is missing a button.
       (셔츠 단추 하나가 없어졌어.)
    G: Oh, is this blue button yours?
       (오, 이 파란색 단추 네 거니?)
    B: No, it isn't. (아니, 그렇지 않아.)
    G: What color is your button?
       (네 단추는 무슨 색이니?)
    B: It's green. (초록색이야.)

  3 W: May I help you? (도와드릴까요?)
    B: Yes, please. I lost my bike.
       (네. 저는 자전거를 잃어버렸어요.)
    W: What color is your bike?
       (당신의 자전거는 무슨 색인가요?)
    B: It's blue. (파란색이에요.)
    W: Sorry, but we only have a red one and a
       yellow one here.
       (죄송하지만, 여기에는 빨간색과 노란색 자전거만 있
       어요.)

UNIT TEST

1　ⓐ yellow (노란색의)　　ⓑ green (초록색의)
　　ⓒ red (빨간색의)　　　ⓓ blue (파란색의)

2　ⓐ It's yellow. (그것은 노란색이다.)
　　ⓑ It's blue. (그것은 파란색이다.)
　　ⓒ It's a triangle. (그것은 삼각형이다.)
　　ⓓ It's a rectangle. (그것은 직사각형이다.)

3　ⓐ The clock is a circle. (시계는 원형이다.)
　　ⓑ The clock is a rectangle. (시계는 직사각형이다.)
　　ⓒ The mirror is a square. (거울은 정사각형이다.)
　　ⓓ The mirror is a circle. (거울은 원형이다.)

4　G: My shirt is missing a button.
　　　(셔츠 단추 하나가 없어졌어.)
　　B: Oh, is this yellow button yours?
　　　(오, 이 노란색 단추 네 거니?)
　　G: No, it isn't. (아니, 그렇지 않아.)
　　B: What color is your button?
　　　(네 단추는 무슨 색이니?)
　　G: It's red. (빨간색이야.)

5　B: There's an eraser over there. It's a rectangle.
　　　Is it yours?
　　　(저기 지우개가 하나 있는데. 직사각형이야.
　　　저거 네 거니?)
　　G: Is the eraser yellow? (그 지우개는 노란색이니?)
　　B: _____
　　ⓐ No, it's yellow. (아니, 노란색이야.)
　　ⓑ Yes, it's a triangle. (응, 삼각형이야.)
　　ⓒ Yes, it is. (응, 그래.)
　　ⓓ No, it's a circle. (아니, 원형이야.)

6　ⓐ W: May I help you? (도와드릴까요?)
　　　B: Yes, please. I lost my bike.
　　　　(네. 저는 자전거를 잃어버렸어요.)
　　ⓑ G: Is your mirror a circle? (네 거울은 원형이니?)
　　　B: No, it isn't. It's red.
　　　　(아니, 그렇지 않아. 그것은 빨간색이야.)
　　ⓒ G: What color is it? (그것은 무슨 색이니?)
　　　B: It's green. (초록색이야.)
　　ⓓ G: Is this your eraser? (이거 네 지우개니?)
　　　B: No, it isn't. My eraser is a square.
　　　　(아니, 그렇지 않아. 내 지우개는 정사각형이야.)

7　M: May I help you? (도와드릴까요?)
　　G: Yes, please. I lost my backpack.
　　　(네. 저는 책가방을 잃어버렸어요.)
　　M: What color is your backpack?
　　　(당신의 책가방은 무슨 색인가요?)
　　G: It's blue. (파란색이에요.)

M: Sorry, but we only have a yellow one and a
　　green one here.
　　(죄송하지만, 여기에는 노란색과 초록색 책가방만 있어
　　요.)
Question: Which one is the girl's backpack?
　　　　(어느 것이 소녀의 책가방인가?)

8　B: Are you ready for Dad's birthday party?
　　　(아빠 생신 파티 준비됐니?)
　　G: Yes, I have a chocolate cake. Dad likes
　　　chocolate cake.
　　　(응, 초콜릿 케이크가 있어. 아빠는 초콜릿 케이크를 좋아
　　　하셔.)
　　B: Good! What shape is it?
　　　(잘했어! 그것은 무슨 모양이니?)
　　G: It's a circle. (원형이야.)
Question: What shape is the cake for Dad?
　　　　(아빠를 위한 케이크는 무슨 모양인가?)

UNIT 2 EVERYDAY LIFE

ANSWERS

P.16

P.18

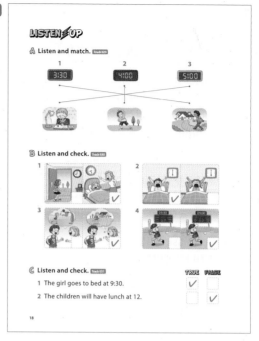

P.17

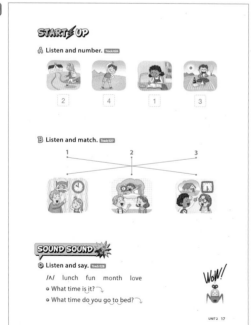

P.19

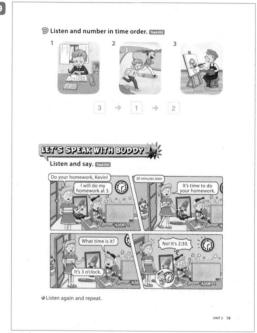

P.20~21 DICTATION

A 1 get   2 home   3 bed
    4 lunch   5 school

B 1 What   2 exercise   3 time
    4 homework   5 have

C 1 get, up, at, 6 (six)
2 to, bed, too, late
3 What, time, have, lunch, after

1 ⓒ 2 ⓒ 3 ⓑ 4 ⓓ
5 ⓐ 6 ⓑ 7 ⓑ 8 ⓓ

SCRIPTS & 해석

P.16 **ARE YOU READY?**

⚡ **Listen and number.**

1 B: Mom, what time is it? (엄마, 몇 시예요?)
   W: It's 7:30. It's time to get up.
   (7시 30분이야. 일어날 시간이야.)

2 G: What time do you go to bed?
   (넌 몇 시에 자니?)
   B: I go to bed at 12 o'clock. (12시에 자.)

⭐ **Listen and repeat.**

get up (일어나다)   go to school (학교에 가다)
have lunch (점심을 먹다)   go home (집에 가다)
exercise (운동하다)
do homework (숙제를 하다)
go to bed (자다)

P.17 **START UP**

Ⓐ **Listen and number.**

1 do homework (숙제를 하다)
2 go to school (학교에 가다)
3 have lunch (점심을 먹다)
4 exercise (운동하다)

Ⓑ **Listen and match.**

1 G: What time is it now? (지금 몇 시야?)
   B: It's 5:30. It's time to go home.
   (5시 30분이야. 집에 갈 시간이야.)

2 B: What time do you get up?
   (넌 몇 시에 일어나니?)
   G: I get up at 8. (8시에 일어나.)

3 G: What time is it? (몇 시예요?)
   M: It's 10 o'clock. It's time to go to bed.
   (10시야. 잘 시간이야.)

P.17 **SOUND SOUND**

⬡ **Listen and say.**

/ʌ/ lunch (점심)   fun (재미있는)
    month (월)   love (사랑)
◐ What time is it? (몇 시야?)
◐ What time do you go to bed? (넌 몇 시에 자니?)

P.18~19 **LISTEN UP**

Ⓐ **Listen and match.**

1 B: What time is it? (몇 시야?)
   G: It's 3:30. (3시 30분이야.)
   B: It's time to go home. (집에 갈 시간이네.)

2 B: What time is it? (몇 시야?)
   G: It's 4 o'clock. (4시야.)
   B: It's time to exercise. (운동할 시간이네.)

3 B: What time is it now? (지금 몇 시야?)
   G: It's 5 o'clock. (5시야.)
   B: It's time to do my homework.
   (숙제 할 시간이네.)

Ⓑ **Listen and check.**

1 W: Get up! It's time to go to school.
   (일어나렴! 학교에 갈 시간이야.)
   G: What time is it? (몇 시예요?)
   W: It's 8:30. You're late. Hurry up.
   (8시 30분이야. 늦었어. 서두르렴.)
   G: Okay. (네.)

2 B: What time do you get up in the morning?
   (넌 아침에 몇 시에 일어나니?)
   G: I get up at 7 o'clock. How about you?
   (7시에 일어나. 너는?)
   B: I get up at 6 o'clock. (난 6시에 일어나.)
   G: Wow, you get up early. (와, 일찍 일어나네.)

3 B: Julie, let's play basketball. (Julie, 농구 하자.)
   G: Sorry, it's time for me to go home.
   (미안, 나 집에 갈 시간이야.)
   B: What time is it? (몇 시인데?)
   G: It's 5:30. My family has dinner at 6 o'clock.
   (5시 30분이야. 우리 가족은 6시에 저녁을 먹어.)
   B: Okay, see you later then.
   (알았어, 그럼 다음에 보자.)

4 G: What do you do after school?
   (넌 방과 후에 무엇을 하니?)
   B: I play baseball at 4. What time is it now?
   (난 4시에 야구를 해. 지금 몇 시야?)

G: It's 3:30. (3시 30분이야.)
B: Oh, I'm late. I have to go now.
(이런, 늦었다. 나 지금 가야 해.)

C Listen and check.

1 G: What time do you go to bed?
(넌 몇 시에 자니?)
B: I go to bed at 11:30. (11시 30분에 자.)
G: Oh, that's too late. (오, 너무 늦네.)
B: How about you? (너는?)
G: I go to bed at 9:30. (난 9시 30분에 자.)

Question: The girl goes to bed at 9:30.
(소녀는 9시 30분에 잔다.)

2 G: What time is it now? (지금 몇 시야?)
B: It's 12 o'clock. (12시야.)
G: Oh, it's time to have lunch.
(오, 점심 먹을 시간이네.)
B: I'm not hungry. Let's play one more game.
(난 배가 고프지 않아. 한 게임만 더 하자.)
G: Okay. Then let's have lunch after that.
(좋아. 그럼 그다음에 점심 먹자.)
B: Sounds good! (좋아!)

Question: The children will have lunch at 12.
(아이들은 12시에 점심을 먹을 것이다.)

D Listen and number in time order.

G: Sam, let's exercise together.
(Sam, 같이 운동하자.)
B: What time is it now? (지금 몇 시야?)
G: It's 3 o'clock. (3시야.)
B: Oh, no. I have art class now!
(오, 이런. 나 지금 미술 수업이 있어!)
G: Then, how about after the class?
(그럼, 그 수업 끝나고는 어때?)
B: I do my homework at 4.
(4시에는 숙제를 해.)
G: You're very busy. (너 정말 바쁘구나.)
B: Let's exercise at 5. (5시에 운동하자.)
G: That sounds good. See you then.
(좋아. 그때 보자.)

P.19 LET'S SPEAK WITH BUDDY

Listen and say.

Ann: Do your homework, Kevin!
(Kevin, 숙제 해야지!)
Kevin: I will do my homework at 3.
(3시에 숙제 할 거야.)

30 minutes later (30분 후)
Ann: It's time to do your homework.
(숙제 할 시간이야.)

Kevin: What time is it? (몇 시인데?)
Ann: It's 3 o'clock. (3시야.)

Kevin: No! It's 2:30. (아니야! 2시 30분이잖아.)

P.20~21 DICTATION

A
1 get up (일어나다)
2 go home (집에 가다)
3 go to bed (자다)
4 have lunch (점심을 먹다)
5 go to school (학교에 가다)

B
1 What time is it now? (지금 몇 시야?)
2 I exercise at 5:30. (난 5시 30분에 운동해.)
3 It's time to go to bed. (잘 시간이야.)
4 What time do you do your homework?
(넌 몇 시에 숙제 하니?)
5 Let's have lunch after that. (그다음에 점심 먹자.)

C
1 B: What time do you get up in the morning?
(넌 아침에 몇 시에 일어나니?)
G: I get up at 7 o'clock. How about you?
(7시에 일어나. 너는?)
B: I get up at 6 o'clock. (난 6시에 일어나.)
G: Wow, you get up early. (와, 일찍 일어나네.)

2 G: What time do you go to bed?
(넌 몇 시에 자니?)
B: I go to bed at 11:30. (11시 30분에 자.)
G: Oh, that's too late. (오, 너무 늦네.)
B: How about you? (너는?)
G: I go to bed at 9:30. (난 9시 30분에 자.)

3 G: What time is it now? (지금 몇 시야?)
B: It's 12 o'clock. (12시야.)
G: Oh, it's time to have lunch.
(오, 점심 먹을 시간이네.)
B: I'm not hungry. Let's play one more game.
(난 배가 고프지 않아. 한 게임만 더 하자.)
G: Okay. Then let's have lunch after that.
(좋아. 그럼 그다음에 점심 먹자.)
B: Sounds good! (좋아!)

P.22~23 UNIT TEST

1 ⓐ go to school (학교에 가다)

ⓑ go home (집에 가다)
ⓒ have lunch (점심을 먹다)
ⓓ do homework (숙제를 하다)

2 ⓐ It's 4 o'clock. (4시이다.)
　　ⓑ It's 5 o'clock. (5시이다.)
　　ⓒ It's 6 o'clock. (6시이다.)
　　ⓓ It's 7 o'clock. (7시이다.)

3 G: What time do you go to bed? (넌 몇 시에 자니?)
　　B: I go to bed at 12. (난 12시에 자.)
　　G: Oh, that's too late. (오, 너무 늦네.)

4 W: What time does the boy exercise?
　　　　(소년은 몇 시에 운동하는가?)
　　ⓐ He does his homework at 4:30.
　　　　(그는 4시 30분에 숙제를 한다.)
　　ⓑ He exercises at 4:30. (그는 4시 30분에 운동한다.)
　　ⓒ He does his homework at 5:30.
　　　　(그는 5시 30분에 숙제를 한다.)
　　ⓓ He exercises at 5:30. (그는 5시 30분에 운동한다.)

5 B: It's time to go to school. (학교 갈 시간이야.)
　　G: What time is it now? (지금 몇 시야?)
　　B: _____
　　ⓐ It's 8 o'clock. (8시야.)
　　ⓑ Oh, I'm late. (오, 늦었다.)
　　ⓒ I go to school at 8. (난 8시에 학교에 가.)
　　ⓓ Hurry up. (서둘러.)

6 ⓐ G: What time do you have lunch?
　　　　　(넌 몇 시에 점심을 먹니?)
　　　B: I have lunch at 12. (난 12시에 점심을 먹어.)
　　ⓑ G: What time do you get up in the morning?
　　　　　(넌 아침에 몇 시에 일어나니?)
　　　B: It's 7:30 now. (지금 7시 30분이야.)
　　ⓒ G: What time is it? (몇 시야?)
　　　B: It's 5 o'clock. (5시야.)
　　ⓓ G: I get up at 6:30. (난 6시 30분에 일어나.)
　　　B: You get up early. (일찍 일어나네.)

7 B: Mary, let's play baseball. (Mary, 야구 하자.)
　　G: Sorry. It's time for me to go home.
　　　　(미안. 나 집에 갈 시간이야.)
　　B: What time is it? (몇 시인데?)
　　G: It's 6:30. My family has dinner at 7 o'clock.
　　　　(6시 30분이야. 우리 가족은 7시에 저녁을 먹어.)
　　B: Okay, see you later then.
　　　　(알았어, 그럼 다음에 보자.)

　　Question: What will the boy and the girl do next?
　　　　　　(소년과 소녀는 다음에 무엇을 할 것인가?)

8 B: What time do you go to bed? (넌 몇 시에 자니?)
　　G: I go to bed at 9 o'clock. (난 9시에 자.)
　　B: You go to bed early. (일찍 자네.)
　　G: How about you? (너는?)
　　B: I go to bed at 10:30. (난 10시 30분에 자.)

　　Question: What time does the boy go to bed?
　　　　　　(소년은 몇 시에 자는가?)

UNIT 3 FEELINGS

ANSWERS

P.24

P.25

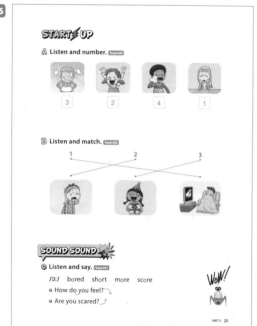

P.26

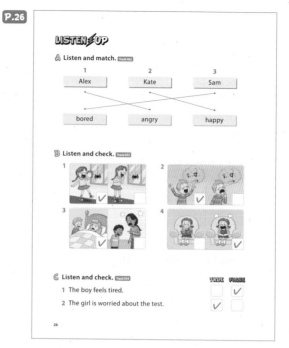

P.27

P.28~29 DICTATION

A 1 i   2 o   3 p, p
   4 a, n   5 e, x

B 1 feel   2 worried   3 sad
   4 scared   5 look

C 1 how, angry
  2 good, scared, worry
  3 happy, bored, tired

1 ⓓ 2 ⓓ 3 ⓐ 4 ⓑ
5 ⓑ 6 ⓒ 7 ⓒ 8 ⓑ

SCRIPTS & 해석

P.24 ARE YOU READY?

⚡ Listen and number.
1 G: Are you scared? (너 무섭니?)
  B: Yes, I am. (응, 무서워.)

2 G: How do you feel? (기분이 어때?)
  B: I'm excited. (신나.)

⭐ Listen and repeat.
happy (행복한)   sad (슬픈)
excited (신이 난)   angry (화난)
scared (무서워하는)   bored (지루한)
worried (걱정하는)   tired (피곤한)

P.25 START UP

Ⓐ Listen and number.
1 bored (지루한)
2 excited (신이 난)
3 angry (화난)
4 sad (슬픈)

Ⓑ Listen and match.
1 G: Are you scared? (너 무섭니?)
  B: Yes, I am. (응, 무서워.)

2 B: You look worried. (너 걱정스러워 보여.)
  G: No, I'm just tired. (아니야, 그냥 피곤해.)

3 B: How do you feel? (기분이 어때?)
  G: I'm happy. Today is my birthday.
     (행복해. 오늘이 내 생일이야.)

P.25 SOUND SOUND

🔊 Listen and say.
/ɔː/ bored (지루한)   short (짧은)
     more (더 많은; 더 많이)   score (점수)
● How do you feel? (기분이 어때?)
● Are you scared? (너 무섭니?)

P.26~27 LISTEN UP

Ⓐ Listen and match.
1 G: Alex, how do you feel? (Alex, 기분이 어때?)
  B: I'm so angry. It's noisy outside. I can't sleep.
     (너무 화가 나. 밖이 시끄러워. 잠을 잘 수가 없어.)

2 B: Kate, how do you feel today?
     (Kate, 오늘 기분이 어때?)
  G: I'm so happy. The weather is so nice.
     (정말 행복해. 날씨가 정말 좋아.)

3 G: Sam, how do you feel today?
     (Sam, 오늘 기분이 어때?)
  B: I feel bored. (지루해.)
  G: Let's play outside. (밖에서 놀자.)

Ⓑ Listen and check.
1 B: Are you okay? You don't look good.
     (너 괜찮니? 안색이 안 좋아 보여.)
  G: Look over there! There's a spider. I'm so
     scared. (저기 좀 봐! 거미가 있어. 너무 무서워.)
  B: Don't worry. I'll take it outside.
     (걱정하지 마. 내가 밖으로 내보낼게.)
  G: Thank you. (고마워.)

2 G: How do you feel? (기분이 어때?)
  B: I'm excited. I have a soccer game today.
     (신나. 난 오늘 축구 경기가 있어.)
  G: Sounds fun! Can I join you?
     (재미있겠다! 나도 같이 해도 되니?)
  B: Of course. (물론이지.)

3 G: How do you feel today? You look sad.
     (오늘 기분이 어때? 슬퍼 보여.)
  B: My mom is sick. (엄마가 편찮으셔.)
  G: I'm sorry to hear that. Don't worry. She will
     be okay.
     (유감이구나. 걱정하지 마. 괜찮아지실 거야.)
  B: Thank you. (고마워.)

4 B: Are you angry? (너 화났니?)
  G: Yes, my dog is so noisy. I can't read my book.
     (응, 우리 개가 너무 시끄러워. 책을 읽을 수가 없어.)

B: Then let's go outside and ride our bikes.
(그럼 밖에 나가서 자전거 타자.)
G: Okay. (그래.)

C Listen and check.

1 **G:** How do you feel today? (오늘 기분이 어때?)
  B: I'm happy. How about you?
  (행복해. 너는 어때?)
  G: I feel bored. (지루해.)
  B: Let's go out. It's a beautiful day!
  (밖에 나가자. 날씨가 정말 좋아!)
  G: Sorry, but I'm too tired.
  (미안하지만, 난 너무 피곤해.)

  Question: The boy feels tired. (소년은 피곤하다.)

2 **B:** Hey, Lisa. Are you okay? You don't look
  good. (얘, Lisa. 너 괜찮니? 안색이 안 좋아 보여.)
  G: I have a big test tomorrow. I'm so worried.
  (내일 중요한 시험이 있어. 너무 걱정돼.)
  B: Don't worry. You can do it.
  (걱정하지 마. 넌 할 수 있어.)
  G: Thanks. (고마워.)

  Question: The girl is worried about the test.
  (소녀는 시험에 대해 걱정한다.)

D Listen and choose.

1 **G:** How do you feel? (기분이 어때?)
  B: I'm bored. I don't like this movie. How
  about you, Elly?
  (지루해. 난 이 영화를 좋아하지 않아. 너는 어때,
  Elly?)
  G: I'm bored, too. (나도 지루해.)
  B: Okay, let's go out and do something.
  (그래, 밖에 나가서 다른 걸 하자.)

2 **G:** Josh, look over there! (Josh, 저기 좀 봐!)
  B: Oh, there's a roller coaster.
  (오, 롤러코스터가 있네.)
  G: Let's ride it. (저거 타자.)
  B: That's a good idea. (좋은 생각이야.)
  G: Are you excited? (신나니?)
  B: Yes, I am. (응, 신나.)

P.27 LET'S SPEAK WITH BUDDY

Listen and say.

Jack: How do you feel today? (오늘 기분이 어때?)
Ann: I'm happy. It's a beautiful day!
(행복해. 날씨가 정말 좋아!)

Ann: How about you? (너는 어때?)

Jack: I'm stressed. (스트레스 받아.)

Ann: Why? (왜?)

Jack: All the girls like me.
(모든 여자애들이 나를 좋아해.)

P.28~29 DICTATION

A 1 tired (피곤한)
  2 bored (지루한)
  3 happy (행복한)
  4 angry (화난)
  5 excited (신이 난)

B 1 How do you feel today? (오늘 기분이 어때?)
  2 I'm so worried. (난 너무 걱정돼.)
  3 I feel sad. (난 슬퍼.)
  4 Are you scared? (너 무섭니?)
  5 You look happy. (너 행복해 보여.)

C 1 **G:** Alex, how do you feel? (Alex, 기분이 어때?)
  B: I'm so angry. It's noisy outside. I can't sleep.
  (너무 화가 나. 밖이 시끄러워. 잠을 잘 수가 없어.)

  2 **B:** Are you okay? You don't look good.
  (너 괜찮니? 안색이 안 좋아 보여.)
  G: Look over there! There's a spider. I'm so
  scared. (저기 좀 봐! 거미가 있어. 너무 무서워.)
  B: Don't worry. I'll take it outside.
  (걱정하지 마. 내가 밖으로 내보낼게.)
  G: Thank you. (고마워.)

  3 **G:** How do you feel today? (오늘 기분이 어때?)
  B: I'm happy. How about you?
  (행복해. 너는 어때?)
  G: I feel bored. (지루해.)
  B: Let's go out. It's a beautiful day!
  (밖에 나가자. 날씨가 정말 좋아!)
  G: Sorry, but I'm too tired.
  (미안하지만, 난 너무 피곤해.)

P.30~31 UNIT TEST

1 ⓐ happy (행복한)   ⓑ bored (지루한)
  ⓒ scared (무서워하는)   ⓓ angry (화난)

2 ⓐ The boy is sad. (소년은 슬프다.)
  ⓑ The girl is happy. (소녀는 행복하다.)
  ⓒ The boy is worried. (소년은 걱정스럽다.)

ⓓ The girl is tired. (소녀는 피곤하다.)

3　G: How do you feel? (기분이 어때?)
　　B: I'm excited. How about you? (신나. 너는 어때?)
　　G: I'm scared. (난 무서워.)

4　W: How does the boy feel? (소년의 기분은 어떠한가?)
　　ⓐ He feels angry. (그는 화가 난다.)
　　ⓑ He feels bored. (그는 지루하다.)
　　ⓒ He feels happy. (그는 행복하다.)
　　ⓓ He feels excited. (그는 신이 난다.)

5　B: How do you feel today? (오늘 기분이 어때?)
　　G: I'm happy. It's a beautiful day. How about
　　　 you? (행복해. 날씨가 정말 좋아. 너는 어때?)
　　B: _____
　　ⓐ Let's go out. (밖에 나가자.)
　　ⓑ I'm happy, too. (나도 행복해.)
　　ⓒ Don't worry. (걱정하지 마.)
　　ⓓ No, I'm not. (아니, 그렇지 않아.)

6　ⓐ G: You don't look good. (너 안색이 안 좋아 보여.)
　　　 B: I feel sad. (난 슬퍼.)
　　ⓑ G: Are you happy? (너 행복하니?)
　　　 B: Yes, I am. (응, 행복해.)
　　ⓒ G: How do you feel? (기분이 어때?)
　　　 B: I'm sorry to hear that. (유감이구나.)
　　ⓓ G: You look worried. (너 걱정스러워 보여.)
　　　 B: No, I'm just tired. (아니야, 그냥 피곤해.)

7　G: How do you feel today? You look excited.
　　　 (오늘 기분이 어때? 신나 보여.)
　　B: I am. I have a soccer game today.
　　　 (응. 난 오늘 축구 경기가 있어.)
　　G: Sounds fun! Can I join you?
　　　 (재미있겠다! 나도 같이 해도 되니?)
　　B: Of course. (물론이지.)
　　G: I'm so excited. (정말 신나.)

　　Question: How does the girl feel?
　　　　　　 (소녀의 기분은 어떠한가?)

8　G: Are you okay? You don't look good.
　　　 (너 괜찮니? 안색이 안 좋아 보여.)
　　B: My dad is sick. I'm so sad.
　　　 (아빠가 편찮으셔. 너무 슬퍼.)
　　G: I'm sorry to hear that. Don't worry. He will be
　　　 okay. (유감이구나. 걱정하지 마. 괜찮아지실 거야.)
　　B: Thanks. (고마워.)

　　Question: The boy feels sad. (소년은 슬프다.)

REVIEW TEST 1 UNITS 1~3

1 ⓓ	2 ⓑ	3 ⓑ	4 ⓑ	5 ⓐ
6 ⓓ	7 ⓒ	8 ⓐ	9 ⓓ	10 ⓒ

1　ⓐ sad (슬픈)
　　ⓑ bored (지루한)
　　ⓒ angry (화난)
　　ⓓ happy (행복한)

2　ⓐ get up (일어나다)
　　ⓑ go home (집에 가다)
　　ⓒ have lunch (점심을 먹다)
　　ⓓ go to bed (자다)

3　G: There's a ruler over there. It's a triangle.
　　　 (저기 자가 하나 있는데. 삼각형이야.)
　　B: What color is it? (그것은 무슨 색이니?)
　　G: It's green. (초록색이야.)
　　B: Oh, that's mine. Thanks. (오, 그거 내 거야. 고마워.)

4　B: What time do you go to bed?
　　　 (너는 몇 시에 자니?)
　　G: I go to bed at 9. How about you?
　　　 (9시에 자. 너는?)
　　B: _____
　　ⓐ It's 9 o'clock. (9시야.)
　　ⓑ I go to bed at 10:30. (난 10시 30분에 자.)
　　ⓒ You go to bed early. (너 일찍 자는구나.)
　　ⓓ It's time to go to bed. (잘 시간이야.)

5　B: Let's ride the roller coaster.
　　　 (롤러코스터 타자.)
　　G: Sorry, but I can't. (미안하지만, 난 못 타.)
　　B: Are you scared? (너 무섭니?)
　　G: _____
　　ⓐ Yes, I am. (응, 무서워.)
　　ⓑ I'm excited, too. (나도 신나.)
　　ⓒ You don't look good. (너 안색이 안 좋아 보여.)
　　ⓓ No, I'm scared. (아니, 무서워.)

6　ⓐ B: What shape is it? (그것은 무슨 모양이니?)
　　　 G: It's a square. (정사각형이야.)
　　ⓑ B: Are you okay? You don't look good.
　　　　 (너 괜찮니? 안색이 안 좋아 보여.)
　　　 G: I feel worried. My mom is sick.
　　　　 (난 걱정돼. 엄마가 편찮으셔.)
　　ⓒ B: What time is it? (몇 시니?)
　　　 G: It's 7 o'clock. (7시야.)
　　ⓓ B: Is your eraser blue? (네 지우개는 파란색이니?)
　　　 G: No, it's a circle. (아니, 원형이야.)

7 ⓐ **G:** Are you sad? (너 슬프니?)
　B: No, I'm just tired. (아니, 그냥 피곤해.)
ⓑ **G:** What color is it? (그것은 무슨 색이니?)
　B: It's red. (빨간색이야.)
ⓒ **G:** What time do you go to school?
　　(너는 몇 시에 학교에 가니?)
　B: It's time to go to school.
　　(학교에 갈 시간이야.)
ⓓ **G:** How do you feel? (기분이 어때?)
　B: I'm bored. (지루해.)

8 **G:** How do you feel today? (오늘 기분이 어때?)
　B: I'm excited. I have a baseball game today. How about you, Kate?
　　(신나. 난 오늘 야구 경기가 있어. Kate, 너는 어때?)
　G: I'm so worried. I have a big test tomorrow.
　　(난 너무 걱정돼. 내일 중요한 시험이 있어.)
　B: Don't worry. You can do it.
　　(걱정하지 마. 넌 할 수 있어.)

　Question: Which girl is Kate?
　　　　　(어느 소녀가 Kate인가?)

9 **G:** John, let's exercise together.
　　(John, 같이 운동하자.)
　B: What time is it now? (지금 몇 시니?)
　G: It's 3 o'clock. (3시야.)
　B: Sorry, I have art class at 3:30.
　　(미안해, 난 3시 30분에 미술 수업이 있어.)
　G: How about at 4:30? (4시 30분은 어때?)
　B: Okay, see you then. (알겠어, 그때 보자.)

　Question: What time will they exercise?
　　　　　(그들은 몇 시에 운동할 것인가?)

10 **W:** Are you ready for school?
　　(학교 갈 준비 됐니?)
　G: Not yet. I can't find my mirror.
　　(아직이요. 거울을 못 찾겠어요.)
　W: What shape is it? Is it a rectangle?
　　(그것은 무슨 모양이니? 직사각형이니?)
　G: No, it's not. It's a circle.
　　(아뇨, 그렇지 않아요. 원형이에요.)
　W: Oh, here it is. (오, 여기 있구나.)
　G: Thanks, Mom. (고마워요, 엄마.)

　Question: What shape is the girl's mirror?
　　　　　(소녀의 거울은 무슨 모양인가?)

UNIT 4 BODY PARTS

ANSWERS

P.34

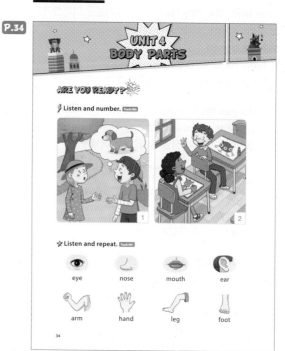

P.35

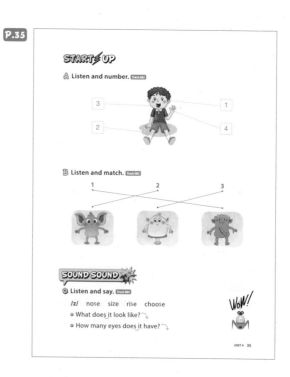

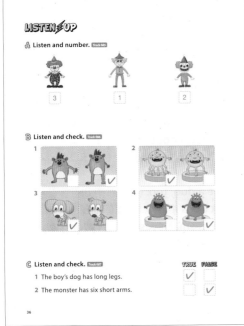

LISTEN UP

A Listen and number. Track 065

3   1   2

B Listen and check. Track 066

1   ✓ (right)
2   ✓ (left)
3   ✓ (left)
4   ✓ (right)

C Listen and check. Track 067

	TRUE	FALSE
1 The boy's dog has long legs.	✓	
2 The monster has six short arms.		✓

36

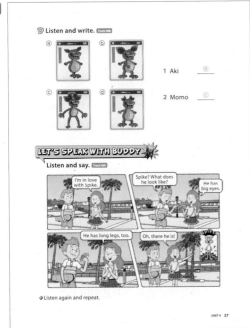

D Listen and write. Track 068

ⓐ ⓑ ⓒ ⓓ

1 Aki   ___ⓐ
2 Momo   ___ⓒ

LET'S SPEAK WITH BUDDY

Listen and say. Track 069

I'm in love with Spike.

Spike? What does he look like?

He has big eyes.

He has long legs, too.

Oh, there he is!

↻ Listen again and repeat.

UNIT 4   37

DICTATION

A 1 e   2 e, a   3 s
4 o, o   5 t, h

B 1 look   2 arms   3 hands
4 eyes   5 small

C 1 big, mouth, foot
2 How, many, five, legs
3 eyes, look, like, ears

UNIT TEST

1 ⓑ   2 ⓓ   3 ⓑ   4 ⓒ
5 ⓓ   6 ⓐ   7 ⓐ   8 ⓒ

SCRIPTS & 해석

ARE YOU READY?

⚡ **Listen and number.**
1 G: What does your dog look like?
(너희 개는 어떻게 생겼니?)
B: She has big ears and short legs.
(귀가 크고 다리가 짧아.)

2 G: How many eyes does your monster have?
(네 괴물은 눈이 몇 개니?)
B: It has three eyes. (세 개야.)

☆ **Listen and repeat.**
eye (눈)   nose (코)   mouth (입)   ear (귀)
arm (팔)   hand (손)   leg (다리)   foot (발)

START UP

A **Listen and number.**
1 eye (눈)
2 leg (다리)
3 mouth (입)
4 hand (손)

B **Listen and match.**
1 G: How many arms does it have?
(그것은 팔이 몇 개니?)
B: It has three arms. (세 개야.)

2 G: What does it look like? (그것은 어떻게 생겼니?)
B: It has big ears. (귀가 커.)

3 G: How many feet does it have?
(그것은 발이 몇 개니?)
B: It has one foot. (한 개야.)

SOUND SOUND

🔊 **Listen and say.**

/z/ nose (코)   size (크기)

rise (오르다)   choose (선택하다)

○ What does it look like? (그것은 어떻게 생겼니?)

○ How many eyes does it have?
(그것은 눈이 몇 개니?)

LISTEN UP

Ⓐ **Listen and number.**

1 **B:** What does he look like? (그는 어떻게 생겼니?)
   G: He has a small nose and long arms.
   (코가 작고 팔이 길어.)

2 **B:** What does he look like? (그는 어떻게 생겼니?)
   G: He has a big mouth and short legs.
   (입이 크고 다리가 짧아.)

3 **G:** What does he look like? (그는 어떻게 생겼니?)
   B: He has small eyes and big feet.
   (눈이 작고 발이 커.)

Ⓑ **Listen and check.**

1 **G:** Wow! Look at him. (와! 그를 좀 봐.)
   B: I can't see him well. What does he look like?
   (난 잘 보이지 않아. 그는 어떻게 생겼니?)
   G: He has short arms and small hands.
   (팔이 짧고 손이 작아.)

2 **B:** The monster has many legs.
   (그 괴물은 다리가 많아.)
   G: How many legs does it have? (다리가 몇 개니?)
   B: It has five legs. (다섯 개야.)
   G: Are you sure? (확실하니?)
   B: Yes, I am. (응, 그래.)

3 **G:** I have a new pet dog, Coco.
   (나에게 새 애완견 Coco가 생겼어.)
   B: What does Coco look like?
   (Coco는 어떻게 생겼니?)
   G: She has big ears. (귀가 커.)
   B: Does she have big eyes, too? (눈도 크니?)
   G: Yes, she does. She's so cute.
   (응, 그래. 정말 귀여워.)

4 **B:** Look at that! It looks strange.
   (저것 좀 봐! 이상하게 생겼어.)
   G: Yes, it does. It has a big mouth.
   (응, 그렇네. 입이 크네.)

   B: And it has three small feet.
   (그리고 세 개의 작은 발을 가지고 있어.)
   G: It looks funny. (웃기게 생겼다.)

Ⓒ **Listen and check.**

1 **B:** Do you have any pets?
   (넌 애완동물을 기르니?)
   G: Yes, I have a dog. He has big eyes and short
   legs. How about you?
   (응, 개 한 마리를 길러. 그는 눈이 크고 다리가 짧아.
   너는 어때?)
   B: I have a dog, too. (나도 개 한 마리를 길러.)
   G: What does it look like? (그것은 어떻게 생겼니?)
   B: She has small eyes and very long legs.
   (눈이 작고 다리가 아주 길어.)

   Question: The boy's dog has long legs.
   (소년의 개는 다리가 길다.)

2 **B:** Look at the monster. (저 괴물 좀 봐.)
   G: I can't see it well. What does it look like?
   (난 잘 보이지 않아. 그것은 어떻게 생겼니?)
   B: It has a long nose and many short arms.
   (긴 코와 많은 짧은 팔을 가지고 있어.)
   G: How many arms does it have? (팔이 몇 개니?)
   B: It has six arms. (여섯 개야.)
   G: Are you sure? (확실하니?)
   B: Oh, sorry. It has five arms. (오, 미안. 다섯 개야.)

   Question: The monster has six short arms.
   (괴물은 여섯 개의 짧은 팔을 가지고 있다.)

Ⓓ **Listen and write.**

1 **G:** My favorite monster is Aki.
   (내가 가장 좋아하는 괴물은 Aki야.)
   B: What does it look like? (그것은 어떻게 생겼니?)
   G: It has one short leg and a big foot.
   (한 개의 짧은 다리와 큰 발을 가지고 있어.)
   B: Does it have big hands? (손이 크니?)
   G: No, it has two small hands.
   (아니, 두 개의 작은 손을 가지고 있어.)

2 **B:** I like the monster, Momo.
   (난 괴물 Momo를 좋아해.)
   G: What does it look like? (그것은 어떻게 생겼니?)
   B: It has many big ears. (큰 귀를 많이 가지고 있어.)
   G: How many ears does it have? (귀가 몇 개니?)
   B: It has four ears. (네 개야.)

LET'S SPEAK WITH BUDDY

🎧 **Listen and say.**

Jenny: I'm in love with Spike.
(난 Spike와 사랑에 빠졌어.)

Jack: Spike? What does he look like?
(Spike? 그는 어떻게 생겼니?)
Jenny: He has big eyes. (눈이 커.)

Jenny: He has long legs, too. (다리도 길어.)

Jenny: Oh, there he is! (오, 저기 그가 있어!)

P.38~39 **DICTATION**

A 1 leg (다리)
2 ear (귀)
3 nose (코)
4 foot (발)
5 mouth (입)

B 1 What does it look like? (그것은 어떻게 생겼니?)
2 It has short arms. (그것은 팔이 짧아.)
3 Does it have big hands? (그것은 손이 크니?)
4 How many eyes does it have?
(그것은 눈이 몇 개니?)
5 It has three small feet.
(그것은 세 개의 작은 발을 가지고 있어.)

C 1 B: Look at that! It looks strange.
(저것 좀 봐! 이상하게 생겼어.)
G: Yes, it does. It has a big mouth.
(응, 그렇네. 입이 크네.)
B: And it has a small foot.
(그리고 한 개의 작은 발을 가지고 있어.)
G: It looks funny. (웃기게 생겼다.)

2 B: The monster has many legs.
(그 괴물은 다리가 많아.)
G: How many legs does it have? (다리가 몇 개니?)
B: It has five legs. (다섯 개야.)
G: Are you sure? (확실하니?)
B: Yes, I am. (응, 그래.)

3 B: Do you have any pets?
(넌 애완동물을 기르니?)
G: Yes, I have a dog. He has big eyes and short legs. How about you?
(응, 개 한 마리를 길러. 그는 눈이 크고 다리가 짧아.
너는 어때?)
B: I have a dog, too. (나도 개 한 마리를 길러.)

G: What does it look like? (그것은 어떻게 생겼니?)
B: She has small eyes and very big ears.
(눈이 작고 귀가 아주 커.)

P.40~41 **UNIT TEST**

1 ⓐ eye (눈)   ⓑ nose (코)
ⓒ mouth (입)   ⓓ ear (귀)

2 ⓐ It has two ears. (그것은 두 개의 귀를 가지고 있다.)
ⓑ It has two feet. (그것은 두 개의 발을 가지고 있다.)
ⓒ It has four hands. (그것은 네 개의 손을 가지고 있다.)
ⓓ It has four feet. (그것은 네 개의 발을 가지고 있다.)

3 B: Look at him! He has long arms.
(그를 좀 봐! 그는 팔이 길어.)
G: Oh, he has long legs, too. (오, 그는 다리도 길어.)
B: He looks funny. (웃기게 생겼다.)

4 W: What does it look like? (그것은 어떻게 생겼는가?)
ⓐ It has four small eyes.
(그것은 네 개의 작은 눈을 가지고 있다.)
ⓑ It has two small hands.
(그것은 두 개의 작은 손을 가지고 있다.)
ⓒ It has two big eyes.
(그것은 두 개의 큰 눈을 가지고 있다.)
ⓓ It has four big hands.
(그것은 네 개의 큰 손을 가지고 있다.)

5 B: The monster has a small mouth and many short legs.
(그 괴물은 작은 입과 많은 짧은 다리를 가지고 있어.)
G: How many legs does it have? (다리가 몇 개니?)
B: _____
ⓐ It has many legs. (그것은 다리가 많아.)
ⓑ It has one leg. (그것은 다리가 한 개야.)
ⓒ It has short legs. (그것은 다리가 짧아.)
ⓓ It has six legs. (그것은 다리가 여섯 개야.)

6 ⓐ G: Does it have big ears? (그것은 귀가 크니?)
B: Yes, it has small ears. (응, 그것은 귀가 작아.)
ⓑ G: What does it look like? (그것은 어떻게 생겼니?)
B: It has a big mouth and three small feet.
(큰 입과 세 개의 작은 발을 가지고 있어.)
ⓒ G: How many eyes does it have?
(그것은 눈이 몇 개니?)
B: It has one eye. (한 개야.)
ⓓ G: Does she have short legs?
(그녀는 다리가 짧니?)
B: No, she has long legs. (아니, 다리가 길어.)

7 **B**: I have a dog. (난 개 한 마리를 길러.)

    G: What does it look like? (그것은 어떻게 생겼니?)

    B: He has big eyes and short legs.
       (눈이 크고 다리가 짧아.)

    G: Does he have big ears? (귀가 크니?)

    B: Yes, he does. He's so cute. (응, 그래. 정말 귀여워.)

    Question: Which one is the boy's dog?
                (어느 것이 소년의 개인가?)

8 **G**: Look at the monster. (저 괴물 좀 봐.)

    B: I can't see it well. What does it look like?
       (난 잘 보이지 않아. 그것은 어떻게 생겼니?)

    G: It has one big eye and many long arms.
       (한 개의 큰 눈과 많은 긴 팔을 가지고 있어.)

    B: How many arms does it have? (팔이 몇 개니?)

    G: It has five arms. (다섯 개야.)

    B: Are you sure? (확실하니?)

    G: Yes, I am. (응, 그래.)

    Question: How many arms does the monster
              have? (괴물은 팔이 몇 개인가?)

UNIT 5 AT HOME

ANSWERS

P.42

P.43
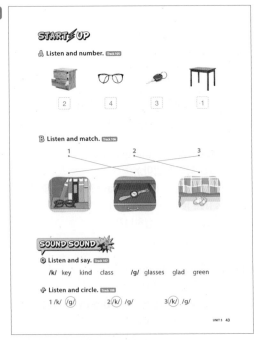

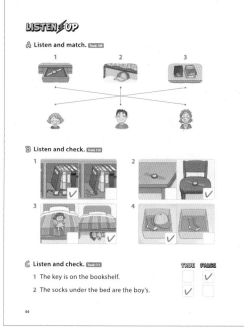

P.46~47 DICTATION

Ⓐ 1 k   2 a, w   3 c, h
   4 c, k   5 e, l

Ⓑ 1 Where   2 glasses   3 bed
   4 Whose   5 on

Ⓒ 1 Where, watch, under
   2 key, bookshelf, in
   3 glasses, table, mine, on

P.48~49 UNIT TEST

1 ⓓ   2 ⓑ   3 ⓐ   4 ⓑ
5 ⓑ   6 ⓓ   7 ⓒ   8 ⓒ

SCRIPTS & 해석

P.42 ARE YOU READY?

⚡ **Listen and number.**

1   M: Honey, where is my car key?
     (여보, 내 자동차 열쇠 어디에 있어요?)
     W: It's in the drawer. (서랍 안에 있어요.)

2   G: Whose socks are these? (이거 누구 양말이니?)
     B: Oh, they are mine. (오, 그거 내 거야.)

3   W: Where are my glasses? (내 안경이 어디 있지?)
     B: They're on the table. (탁자 위에 있어요.)

☆ **Listen and repeat.**

key (열쇠)	watch (손목시계)
socks (양말)	glasses (안경)
bed (침대)	table (탁자)
drawer (서랍)	bookshelf (책꽂이)

P.43 START UP

Ⓐ **Listen and number.**

1 table (탁자)
2 drawer (서랍)
3 key (열쇠)
4 glasses (안경)

Ⓑ **Listen and match.**

1   B: Where is my watch? (내 손목시계가 어디 있지?)
     G: It's in the drawer. (서랍 안에 있어.)

2   G: Where are my socks? (내 양말이 어디 있지?)
     B: They're under the bed. (침대 밑에 있어.)

3   B: Where are my glasses? (내 안경이 어디 있지?)
     G: They're on the bookshelf. (책꽂이 위에 있어.)

SOUND SOUND

🔵 **Listen and say.**

/k/ key (열쇠)　　kind (친절한)　class (학급, 수업)
/g/ glasses (안경)　glad (기쁜)　green (초록색의)

➕ **Listen and circle.**

1 glad　2 class　3 kind

LISTEN UP

Ⓐ **Listen and match.**

1 B: Whose watch is that? It's in the drawer.
(저거 누구 손목시계니? 서랍 안에 있어.)
G: Oh, that's Grandma's watch.
(오, 그거 할머니 손목시계야.)

2 W: Whose cap is this? It's under the bed.
(이거 누구 모자니? 침대 밑에 있어.)
B: I don't know. (모르겠어요.)
G: It's Uncle John's cap. (그거 John 삼촌 모자예요.)

3 G: Where are my books? (내 책들이 어디 있지?)
B: Whose books are these? They are on the
table. (이것들은 누구 책이니? 탁자 위에 있어.)
G: Oh, they're mine. Thanks.
(오, 그것들은 내 거야. 고마워.)

Ⓑ **Listen and check.**

1 W: Hurry up. You're late. (서두르렴. 늦었구나.)
B: Where are my glasses? (제 안경 어디에 있어요?)
W: Whose glasses are those?
(저건 누구 안경이니?)
B: They are mine. Thank you, Mom.
(그거 제 거예요. 고마워요, 엄마.)

2 B: Where is my watch? (내 손목시계가 어디 있지?)
G: Isn't it on the desk? (책상 위에 없니?)
B: No, it isn't there. (아니, 거기에 없어.)
G: Oh, it's on the chair. (오, 의자 위에 있네.)

3 G: Where is my doll? (제 인형 어디에 있어요?)
M: Whose doll is that? It's under the bed.
(저건 누구 인형이니? 침대 밑에 있구나.)
G: Oh, that's my doll. Thank you, Dad.
(오, 그거 제 인형이에요. 고마워요, 아빠.)
M: Sure. (천만에.)

4 B: Where are my socks? (제 양말 어디에 있어요?)
W: Whose socks are those? They're in the box.
(저건 누구 양말이니? 상자 안에 있구나.)

B: Oh, they're mine. There's my cap, too.
(오, 그거 제 거예요. 제 모자도 있네요.)

Ⓒ **Listen and check.**

1 W: Where is my car key?
(내 자동차 열쇠 어디에 있어요?)
M: Isn't it on the bookshelf? (책꽂이 위에 없어요?)
W: No, it isn't there. (아뇨, 거기 없어요.)
M: Then, how about in the drawer?
(그럼, 서랍 안에는요?)
W: There it is! Thank you for your help.
(거기 있네요! 도와줘서 고마워요.)
Question: The key is on the bookshelf.
(열쇠는 책꽂이 위에 있다.)

2 G: Nick, we're late for school. Hurry up.
(Nick, 우리 학교에 늦었어. 서둘러.)
B: Where are my socks? Where are they?
(내 양말이 어디 있지? 어디에 있는 거야?)
G: Whose socks are those? They're under the
bed. (저건 누구 양말이니? 침대 밑에 있어.)
B: Oh, those are my socks. Thanks.
(오, 저거 내 양말이야. 고마워.)
G: Sure. (천만에.)
Question: The socks under the bed are the
boy's.
(침대 밑에 있는 양말은 소년의 것이다.)

Ⓓ **Listen and write.**

1 B: Where is my ball? (제 공 어디에 있어요?)
W: Isn't it in the box? (상자 안에 없니?)
B: No, it isn't there. (아뇨, 거기 없어요.)
W: Then, how about under the bed?
(그럼, 침대 밑에는?)
B: Oh, there it is! Thank you for your help.
(오, 거기 있네요! 도와주셔서 감사해요.)

2 G: I can't see well. Where are my glasses?
(잘 안 보여요. 제 안경 어디에 있어요?)
W: Whose glasses are those? They're on the
desk. (저건 누구 안경이니? 책상 위에 있구나.)
G: Oh, those aren't mine. They're Dad's
glasses.
(오, 그건 제 게 아니에요. 그건 아빠의 안경이에요.)
W: Then, how about on the bookshelf?
(그럼, 책꽂이 위에는?)
G: Oh, there they are! Thank you, Mom.
(오, 거기 있네요! 고마워요, 엄마.)

LET'S SPEAK WITH BUDDY

🔵 **Listen and say.**

Ann: Where are my books? (내 책들이 어디 있지?)

Mom: Aren't they on the bookshelf?
(책꽂이 위에 없니?)

Ann: No. Where are they? (없어요. 어디에 있는 거지?)

Mom: Whose books are those? They're under the table. (저것들은 누구 책이니? 탁자 밑에 있구나.)

Ann: Oh, those are my books! (오, 제 책들이에요!)

DICTATION

Ⓐ **Listen and write the letters.**

1 key (열쇠)
2 drawer (서랍)
3 watch (손목시계)
4 socks (양말)
5 bookshelf (책꽂이)

Ⓑ **Listen and write the words.**

1 Where is my doll? (내 인형이 어디 있지?)
2 Whose glasses are these? (이거 누구 안경이니?)
3 The ball is under the bed. (공이 침대 밑에 있어.)
4 Whose cap is this? (이거 누구 모자니?)
5 The books are on the table.
(책들이 탁자 위에 있어.)

Ⓒ **Listen and fill in the blanks.**

1 G: Where is my watch?
(제 손목시계 어디에 있어요?)
M: Whose watch is that? It's under the bed.
(저건 누구 손목시계니? 침대 밑에 있구나.)
G: Oh, that is my watch. Thank you, Dad.
(오, 그거 제 손목시계예요. 고마워요, 아빠.)
M: Sure. (천만에.)

2 W: Where is my car key?
(내 자동차 열쇠 어디에 있어요?)
M: Isn't it on the bookshelf? (책꽂이 위에 없어요?)
W: No, it isn't there. (아뇨, 거기 없어요.)
M: Then, how about in the drawer?
(그럼, 서랍 안에는요?)
W: There it is! Thank you for your help.
(거기 있네요! 도와줘서 고마워요.)

3 G: I can't see well. Where are my glasses?
(잘 안 보여요. 제 안경 어디에 있어요?)
W: Whose glasses are those? They're on the

table. (저건 누구 안경이니? 탁자 위에 있구나.)
G: Oh, those aren't mine. They're Dad's glasses.
(오, 그건 제 게 아니에요. 그건 아빠의 안경이에요.)
W: Then, how about on the bookshelf?
(그럼, 책꽂이 위에는?)
G: Oh, there they are! Thank you, Mom.
(오, 거기 있네요! 고마워요, 엄마.)

UNIT TEST

1 ⓐ socks (양말)   ⓑ key (열쇠)
ⓒ watch (손목시계)   ⓓ glasses (안경)

2 ⓐ The watch is on the table.
(손목시계가 탁자 위에 있다.)
ⓑ The key is in the drawer. (열쇠가 서랍 안에 있다.)
ⓒ The books are on the bookshelf.
(책들이 책꽂이 위에 있다.)
ⓓ The socks are under the bed.
(양말이 침대 밑에 있다.)

3 B: Where is my watch? (내 손목시계가 어디 있지?)
G: Whose watch is this? (이건 누구 손목시계니?)
B: Oh, that's mine. Thanks. (오, 그거 내 거야. 고마워.)

4 M: Where is my car key?
(내 자동차 열쇠 어디에 있어요?)
W: Isn't it on the table? (탁자 위에 없어요?)
M: _____
ⓐ Yes, it's under the table. (네, 탁자 밑에 있어요.)
ⓑ No, it isn't there. (아뇨, 거기 없어요.)
ⓒ No, it's my key. (아뇨, 그건 제 열쇠예요.)
ⓓ The key is on the box. (열쇠는 상자 위에 있어요.)

5 G: I can't see well. Where are my glasses?
(잘 안 보여. 내 안경이 어디 있지?)
B: Whose glasses are these? (이건 누구 안경이니?)
G: _____
ⓐ They're on the bookshelf. (그건 책꽂이 위에 있어.)
ⓑ Oh, they're mine. (오, 그거 내 거야.)
ⓒ My glasses are on the desk.
(내 안경은 책상 위에 있어.)
ⓓ No, they're my watches.
(아니, 그것들은 내 손목시계야.)

6 ⓐ G: Where is my book? (내 책이 어디 있지?)
B: I don't know. (모르겠어.)
ⓑ G: Whose watch is this? (이거 누구 손목시계니?)
B: It's Grandma's watch. (그거 할머니 손목시계야.)
ⓒ G: Where are my socks? (내 양말이 어디 있지?)

B: They are in the drawer. (서랍 안에 있어.)

ⓓ G: Isn't it on the desk? (그거 책상 위에 없니?)

B: No, it's mine. (아니, 그건 내 거야.)

7 W: You're late for school. Hurry up.
   (학교에 늦었다. 서두르렴.)

B: Where are my socks? (제 양말 어디에 있어요?)

W: Aren't they in the drawer? (서랍 안에 없니?)

B: No, they aren't. (아뇨, 없어요.)

W: Then, how about on the bed?
   (그럼, 침대 위에는?)

B: Oh, there they are. Thanks, Mom.
   (오, 거기 있네요. 고마워요, 엄마.)

Question: Where are the boy's socks?
         (소년의 양말은 어디에 있는가?)

8 G: Where is my key? (내 열쇠가 어디 있지?)

B: Isn't it on the bookshelf? (책꽂이 위에 없니?)

G: No, that's not mine. It's Dad's car key.
   (아니, 그건 내 게 아니야. 그건 아빠의 자동차 열쇠야.)

B: Whose key is that? It's in the box.
   (저건 누구 열쇠니? 상자 안에 있어.)

G: Oh, that's mine. Thanks. (오, 그거 내 거야. 고마워.)

Question: What is on the bookshelf?
         (책꽂이 위에 무엇이 있는가?)

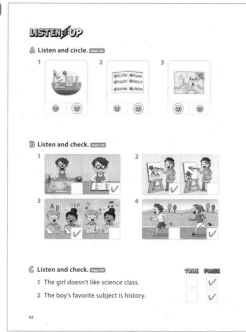

LISTEN UP

A Listen and circle. Track 132

1   2   3

B Listen and check. Track 133

1   2

3   4

C Listen and check. Track 134

	TRUE	FALSE
1 The girl doesn't like science class.		✓
2 The boy's favorite subject is history.		✓

52

D Listen and write. Track 135

MON	TUE	WED	THU	FRI
1				
2				
3				

Name	Favorite Subject
1 Sue	ⓔ
2 Joe	ⓐ
3 Ann	ⓓ

LET'S SPEAK WITH BUDDY

Listen and say. Track 136

What's your favorite subject?

No, it's fun.

My favorite subject is math.

I don't like math. Isn't it hard?

I'm good at math. Let's study together. I can help you.

No thanks.

↻ Listen again and repeat.

UNIT 6   53

DICTATION

A 1 a   2 t, h   3 u, i
4 s, c   5 i, o

B 1 subject   2 like   3 good
4 English   5 interested

C 1 music, like, art
2 favorite, math, fun
3 science, history, Don't, interested

UNIT TEST

1 ⓑ   2 ⓒ   3 ⓐ   4 ⓒ
5 ⓓ   6 ⓑ   7 ⓒ   8 ⓓ

SCRIPTS & 해석

ARE YOU READY?

⚡ **Listen and number.**

1 **B**: What's your favorite subject?
(네가 가장 좋아하는 과목은 뭐니?)
G: My favorite subject is science.
(내가 가장 좋아하는 과목은 과학이야.)

2 **G**: Are you interested in painting?
(너는 그림 그리기에 관심이 있니?)
B: Yes, I am. I like art class.
(응, 있어. 나는 미술 수업을 좋아해.)

⭐ **Listen and repeat.**

art (미술)   music (음악)   English (영어)
math (수학)   science (과학)   P.E. (체육)
history (역사)

START UP

A **Listen and number.**

1 math (수학)
2 P.E. (체육)
3 science (과학)
4 art (미술)

B **Listen and match.**

1 **G**: Eric, what's your favorite subject?
(Eric, 네가 가장 좋아하는 과목은 뭐니?)
B: My favorite subject is English.
(내가 가장 좋아하는 과목은 영어야.)

2 **B**: Amy, are you interested in music?
(Amy, 너는 음악에 관심이 있니?)
G: Yes. I like music class.
(응. 나는 음악 수업을 좋아해.)

23

3 G: Peter, do you like P.E.?
   (Peter, 너는 체육을 좋아하니?)
   B: No, I don't. I like history.
   (아니, 안 좋아해. 나는 역사를 좋아해.)

🔘 **Listen and say.**

Silent C   science (과학)   scissors (가위)
           scene (장면)   muscle (근육)
   ◦ What's your favorite subject?
   (네가 가장 좋아하는 과목은 뭐니?)
   ◦ Are you interested in painting?
   (너는 그림 그리기에 관심이 있니?)

Ⓐ **Listen and circle.**

1 B: Are you interested in science?
   (너는 과학에 관심이 있니?)
   G: No. I don't like science. It's too hard.
   (아니. 나는 과학을 좋아하지 않아. 그건 너무 어려워.)

2 B: Do you like music? (너는 음악을 좋아하니?)
   G: No, I don't. I can't sing well.
   (아니, 안 좋아해. 나는 노래를 잘 못 불러.)

3 B: Are you interested in history?
   (너는 역사에 관심이 있니?)
   G: Yes, I am. It's my favorite subject.
   (응, 있어. 그게 내가 가장 좋아하는 과목이야.)

Ⓑ **Listen and check.**

1 G: What's your favorite subject?
   (네가 가장 좋아하는 과목은 뭐니?)
   B: My favorite subject is math.
   (내가 가장 좋아하는 과목은 수학이야.)
   G: Oh, really? Isn't it hard?
   (오, 정말? 어렵지 않니?)
   B: No, it's fun. (아니, 재미있어.)

2 B: Are you interested in painting?
   (너는 그림 그리기에 관심이 있니?)
   G: Yes, I am. I like art.
   (응, 있어. 나는 미술을 좋아해.)
   B: Are you good at art? (너는 미술을 잘하니?)
   G: Yes, I am. (응, 잘해.)

3 B: What's your favorite subject?
   (네가 가장 좋아하는 과목은 뭐니?)

G: My favorite subject is English. How about
   you? (내가 가장 좋아하는 과목은 영어야. 너는?)
   B: Me, too. I like English a lot.
   (나도. 나는 영어를 정말 좋아해.)
   G: Good. We can study together.
   (잘됐다. 우리 같이 공부할 수 있어.)

4 B: Are you good at P.E.? (너는 체육을 잘하니?)
   G: Yes, it's my favorite subject. How about
   you? (응, 그게 내가 가장 좋아하는 과목이야. 너는?)
   B: I don't like P.E. I'm not good at it.
   (나는 체육을 좋아하지 않아. 나는 그것을 잘 못해.)

Ⓒ **Listen and check.**

1 G: We have science class today.
   (우리 오늘 과학 수업이 있어.)
   B: Oh, no! (오, 이런!)
   G: Don't you like science?
   (너는 과학을 좋아하지 않니?)
   B: No, I don't. It's boring. Do you like science?
   (아니, 안 좋아해. 그건 지루해. 너는 과학을 좋아하
   니?)
   G: Yes. It's fun. (응. 재미있어.)

Question: The girl doesn't like science class.
   (소녀는 과학 수업을 좋아하지 않는다.)

2 G: What's your favorite subject?
   (네가 가장 좋아하는 과목은 뭐니?)
   B: My favorite subject is music. How about
   you? (내가 가장 좋아하는 과목은 음악이야. 너는?)
   G: My favorite subject is history.
   (내가 가장 좋아하는 과목은 역사야.)
   B: Oh, really? (오, 정말?)
   G: Yes. Don't you like history?
   (응. 너는 역사를 좋아하지 않니?)
   B: No, I don't. I'm not interested in it.
   (아니, 안 좋아해. 나는 그것에 관심이 없어.)

Question: The boy's favorite subject is history.
   (소년이 가장 좋아하는 과목은 역사이다.)

Ⓓ **Listen and write.**

1 G: Oh, no! We have music class today.
   (오, 이런! 우리 오늘 음악 수업이 있어.)
   B: Don't you like music, Sue?
   (Sue, 너는 음악을 좋아하지 않니?)
   G: No, I don't. I like art. It's my favorite subject.
   (아니, 안 좋아해. 나는 미술을 좋아해. 그게 내가 가장
   좋아하는 과목이야.)

2 G: Joe, what's your favorite subject?
   (Joe, 네가 가장 좋아하는 과목은 뭐니?)

B: My favorite subject is math.
(내가 가장 좋아하는 과목은 수학이야.)

G: Isn't it hard? (어렵지 않니?)

B: No, it's fun. (아니, 재미있어.)

3 **G**: Are you interested in P.E.?
(너는 체육에 관심이 있니?)

B: Yes. How about you, Ann?
(응. 너는 어때, Ann?)

G: No. I'm not good at P.E.
(난 관심 없어. 나는 체육을 잘 못해.)

B: Then, what's your favorite subject?
(그럼, 네가 가장 좋아하는 과목은 뭐니?)

G: My favorite subject is science.
(내가 가장 좋아하는 과목은 과학이야.)

P.53 **LET'S SPEAK WITH BUDDY**

🔘 **Listen and say.**

Jenny: What's your favorite subject?
(네가 가장 좋아하는 과목은 뭐니?)

Jack: My favorite subject is math.
(내가 가장 좋아하는 과목은 수학이야.)

Jenny: I don't like math. Isn't it hard?
(나는 수학을 좋아하지 않아. 어렵지 않니?)

Jack: No, it's fun. (아니, 재미있어.)

Jack: I'm good at math. Let's study together.
I can help you.
(난 수학을 잘해. 같이 공부하자. 내가 널 도와줄 수 있어.)

Jenny: No thanks. (아니, 괜찮아.)

P.54~55 **DICTATION**

Ⓐ **Listen and write the letters.**

1 art (미술)

2 math (수학)

3 music (음악)

4 science (과학)

5 history (역사)

Ⓑ **Listen and write the words.**

1 What's your favorite subject?
(네가 가장 좋아하는 과목은 뭐니?)

2 Don't you like P.E.? (너는 체육을 좋아하지 않니?)

3 Are you good at art? (너는 미술을 잘하니?)

4 My favorite subject is English.

(내가 가장 좋아하는 과목은 영어야.)

5 Are you interested in painting?
(너는 그림 그리기에 관심이 있니?)

Ⓒ **Listen and fill in the blanks.**

1 **G**: Oh, no! We have music class today.
(오, 이런! 우리 오늘 음악 수업이 있어.)

B: Don't you like music, Sue?
(Sue, 너는 음악을 좋아하지 않니?)

G: No, I don't. I like art. It's my favorite subject.
(아니, 안 좋아해. 나는 미술을 좋아해. 그게 내가 가장 좋아하는 과목이야.)

2 **G**: What's your favorite subject?
(네가 가장 좋아하는 과목은 뭐니?)

B: My favorite subject is math.
(내가 가장 좋아하는 과목은 수학이야.)

G: Oh, really? Isn't it hard?
(오, 정말? 어렵지 않니?)

B: No, it's fun. (아니, 재미있어.)

3 **G**: What's your favorite subject?
(네가 가장 좋아하는 과목은 뭐니?)

B: My favorite subject is science. How about you? (내가 가장 좋아하는 과목은 과학이야. 너는?)

G: My favorite subject is history.
(내가 가장 좋아하는 과목은 역사야.)

B: Oh, really? (오, 정말?)

G: Yes. Don't you like history?
(응. 너는 역사를 좋아하지 않니?)

B: No, I don't. I'm not interested in it.
(아니, 안 좋아해. 나는 그것에 관심이 없어.)

P.56~57 **UNIT TEST**

1 ⓐ music (음악)　　ⓑ history (역사)
ⓒ math (수학)　　ⓓ science (과학)

2 ⓐ He is good at math. (그는 수학을 잘한다.)
ⓑ He isn't good at English.
(그는 영어를 잘하지 못한다.)
ⓒ She is good at English. (그녀는 영어를 잘한다.)
ⓓ She isn't good at math.
(그녀는 수학을 잘하지 못한다.)

3 **G**: Are you interested in music?
(너는 음악에 관심이 있니?)

B: Yes. I like music. How about you?
(응. 나는 음악을 좋아해. 너는?)

G: Me, too. It's my favorite subject.
(나도. 그게 내가 가장 좋아하는 과목이야.)

4 ⓐ **B**: What's your favorite subject?
(네가 가장 좋아하는 과목은 뭐니?)
G: My favorite subject is math.
(내가 가장 좋아하는 과목은 수학이야.)
ⓑ **B**: Are you interested in science?
(너는 과학에 관심이 있니?)
G: No, I'm not. (아니, 관심 없어.)
ⓒ **B**: Do you like math? (너는 수학을 좋아하니?)
G: No, I don't. It's too hard.
(아니, 안 좋아해. 그건 너무 어려워.)
ⓓ **B**: Are you good at science?
(너는 과학을 잘하니?)
G: Yes, I am. (응, 잘해.)

5 **G**: We have P.E. class today.
(우리 오늘 체육 수업이 있어.)
B: Oh, no! (오, 이런!)
G: Don't you like P.E.? (너는 체육을 좋아하지 않니?)
B: _____
ⓐ Yes, I am. (응, 그래.)
ⓑ No, I don't. I like P.E.
(아니, 안 좋아해. 나는 체육을 좋아해.)
ⓒ I'm good at P.E. (나는 체육을 잘해.)
ⓓ No. I'm not interested in it.
(안 좋아해. 나는 그것에 관심이 없어.)

6 ⓐ **G**: Do you like music? (너는 음악을 좋아하니?)
B: No. I can't sing well.
(아니. 나는 노래를 잘 못 불러.)
ⓑ **G**: Are you good at math? (너는 수학을 잘하니?)
B: No, it's fun. (아니, 그건 재미있어.)
ⓒ **G**: What's your favorite subject?
(네가 가장 좋아하는 과목은 뭐니?)
B: My favorite subject is P.E.
(내가 가장 좋아하는 과목은 체육이야.)
ⓓ **G**: Are you interested in painting?
(너는 그림 그리기에 관심이 있니?)
B: Yes. I like art. (응. 나는 미술을 좋아해.)

7 **B**: What's your favorite subject?
(네가 가장 좋아하는 과목은 뭐니?)
G: My favorite subject is math.
(내가 가장 좋아하는 과목은 수학이야.)
B: Oh, really? Isn't it hard? (오, 정말? 어렵지 않니?)
G: No, it isn't. Don't you like math?
(아니, 안 어려워. 너는 수학을 좋아하지 않니?)
B: No. I like science. It's my favorite subject.
(안 좋아해. 나는 과학을 좋아해. 그게 내가 가장 좋아하는 과목이야.)
G: I like it, too. (나도 과학을 좋아해.)

Question: What is the boy's favorite subject?

(소년이 가장 좋아하는 과목은 무엇인가?)

8 **B**: Oh, we have art class today.
(오, 우리 오늘 미술 수업이 있어.)
G: Are you interested in painting?
(너는 그림 그리기에 관심이 있니?)
B: Yes, I like art. How about you?
(응, 나는 미술을 좋아해. 너는?)
G: No. I like history. (안 좋아해. 나는 역사를 좋아해.)
B: Oh, really? (오, 정말?)
G: Yes, I'm interested in it. It's fun.
(응, 나는 역사에 관심이 있어. 그건 재미있어.)

Question: The girl is interested in history.
(소녀는 역사에 관심이 있다.)

P.58~59

REVIEW TEST 2 UNITS 4~6

| 1 ⓐ | 2 ⓒ | 3 ⓑ | 4 ⓒ | 5 ⓓ |
| 6 ⓐ | 7 ⓒ | 8 ⓓ | 9 ⓓ | 10 ⓑ |

1 ⓐ watch (손목시계) ⓑ key (열쇠)
ⓒ glasses (안경) ⓓ socks (양말)

2 ⓐ English (영어) ⓑ math (수학)
ⓒ science (과학) ⓓ history (역사)

3 **B**: Look at that! It looks strange.
(저것 좀 봐! 이상하게 생겼어.)
G: I can't see it well. (난 잘 보이지 않아.)
B: It has one big mouth and many eyes.
(그것은 큰 입과 많은 눈을 가지고 있어.)
G: How many eyes does it have? (눈이 몇 개니?)
B: It has four eyes. (네 개야.)

4 **B**: Where is my key? (내 열쇠가 어디 있지?)
G: Whose key is that? (저건 누구 열쇠니?)
B: _____
ⓐ They're not mine. (그것들은 내 게 아니야.)
ⓑ It's on the table. (탁자 위에 있어.)
ⓒ That is my key. (그거 내 열쇠야.)
ⓓ It isn't there. (거기에 없어.)

5 **B**: Oh, no! We have English class today.
(오, 이런! 우리 오늘 영어 수업이 있어.)
G: Don't you like English?
(너는 영어를 좋아하지 않니?)
B: No, I don't. Do you like it?
(아니, 안 좋아해. 넌 영어를 좋아하니?)
G: _____
ⓐ No, it's fun. (아니, 재미있어.)

ⓑ Yes, I'm interested in art.
(응, 나는 미술에 관심이 있어.)
ⓒ No, I'm not good at P.E.
(아니, 나는 체육을 잘 못해.)
ⓓ Yes, it's my favorite subject.
(응, 그게 내가 가장 좋아하는 과목이야.)

6 ⓐ G: Where are my socks? (내 양말이 어디 있지?)
   B: They're mine. (그것들은 내 거야.)
   ⓑ G: Does it have a big nose? (그것은 코가 크니?)
   B: Yes, it does. (응, 그래.)
   ⓒ G: Are you interested in history?
      (너는 역사에 관심이 있니?)
   B: No. I don't like history.
      (아니. 나는 역사를 좋아하지 않아.)
   ⓓ G: Isn't your watch on the bookshelf?
      (네 손목시계 책꽂이 위에 없니?)
   B: No, it isn't there. (아니, 거기에 없어.)

7 ⓐ B: What does it look like? (그것은 어떻게 생겼니?)
   G: It has big hands and small feet.
      (손이 크고 발이 작아.)
   ⓑ B: Are you good at science? (너는 과학을 잘하니?)
   G: No, it's too hard. (아니, 그건 너무 어려워.)
   ⓒ B: How many legs does it have?
      (그것은 다리가 몇 개니?)
   G: It has long legs. (다리가 길어.)
   ⓓ B: Whose glasses are those? (저거 누구 안경이니?)
   G: They are Grandma's glasses.
      (그거 할머니 안경이야.)

8 G: I can't see well. Where are my glasses?
      (잘 안 보여요. 제 안경 어디에 있어요?)
   W: Aren't they on the desk? (책상 위에 없니?)
   G: No, they aren't. (아뇨, 없어요.)
   W: Then, how about in the drawer?
      (그럼, 서랍 안에는?)
   G: No, they aren't there. Where are they?
      (아뇨, 거기에 없어요. 어디 있어요?)
   W: Hey! They are under the bed.
      (얘! 침대 밑에 있구나.)
   G: Oh, thank you, Mom. (오, 고마워요, 엄마.)

   Question: Where are the girl's glasses?
      (소녀의 안경은 어디에 있는가?)

9 G: My favorite monster is Pepi.
      (내가 가장 좋아하는 괴물은 Pepi야.)
   B: What does it look like? (그것은 어떻게 생겼니?)
   G: It has big ears and long legs.
      (귀가 크고 다리가 길어.)
   B: Does it have long arms, too? (팔도 기니?)

G: No, it has five short arms.
   (아니, 다섯 개의 짧은 팔을 가지고 있어.)

Question: Pepi has big ears and short arms.
   (Pepi는 큰 귀와 짧은 팔을 가지고 있다.)

10 B: Are you interested in music?
      (너는 음악에 관심이 있니?)
   G: Yes. How about you, Joe? (응. 너는 어때, Joe?)
   B: No. I can't sing well.
      (난 관심 없어. 나는 노래를 잘 못 불러.)
   G: Then, what's your favorite subject?
      (그럼, 네가 가장 좋아하는 과목은 뭐니?)
   B: My favorite subject is math.
      (내가 가장 좋아하는 과목은 수학이야.)
   G: Oh, really? Isn't it hard? (오, 정말? 어렵지 않니?)
   B: No, it isn't. It's fun. (아니, 그렇지 않아. 재미있어.)

   Question: The boy's favorite subject is math.
      (소년이 가장 좋아하는 과목은 수학이다.)

UNIT 7 HOBBIES

ANSWERS

P.60

P.61

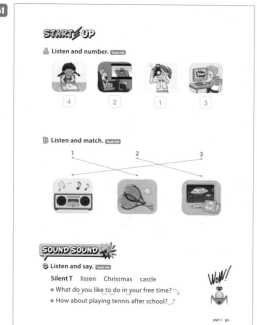

P.62

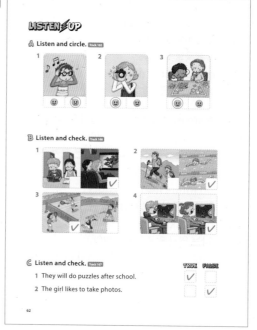

P.63

P.64~65 DICTATION

A 1 tennis   2 photos   3 watch
   4 listen   5 games

B 1 do   2 read   3 puzzles
   4 take   5 swimming

28

C 1 like, play, tennis
  2 puzzles, hobby, How, about
  3 free, time, watch, movie

1 ⓐ 2 ⓒ 3 ⓒ 4 ⓑ
5 ⓒ 6 ⓓ 7 ⓐ 8 ⓓ

SCRIPTS & 해석

P.60 ARE YOU READY?

⚡ Listen and number.

1 G: What do you like to do in your free time?
(너는 여가시간에 무엇을 하는 것을 좋아하니?)
   B: I like to play computer games.
   (나는 컴퓨터 게임 하는 것을 좋아해.)

2 B: How about playing tennis after school?
   (방과 후에 테니스 치는 게 어때?)
   G: That sounds good. (좋은 생각이야.)

☆ Listen and repeat.

listen to music (음악을 듣다)
play tennis (테니스를 치다)
watch movies (영화를 보다)
take photos (사진을 찍다)
play computer games (컴퓨터 게임을 하다)
do puzzles (퍼즐을 맞추다)

P.61 START UP

Ⓐ Listen and number.

1 take photos (사진을 찍다)
2 watch movies (영화를 보다)
3 play computer games (컴퓨터 게임을 하다)
4 do puzzles (퍼즐을 맞추다)

Ⓑ Listen and match.

1 G: What do you like to do after school?
   (너는 방과 후에 무엇을 하는 것을 좋아하니?)
   B: I like to play tennis.
   (나는 테니스 치는 것을 좋아해.)

2 G: Do you like to do puzzles?
   (너는 퍼즐 맞추는 것을 좋아하니?)
   B: No, I like to watch movies.
   (아니, 나는 영화 보는 것을 좋아해.)

3 G: How about listening to music?
   (음악 듣는 게 어때?)
   B: That sounds good. (좋은 생각이야.)

P.61 SOUND SOUND

⬡ Listen and say.

Silent T listen (듣다)   Christmas (크리스마스)
          castle (성)
• What do you like to do in your free time?
  (너는 여가시간에 무엇을 하는 것을 좋아하니?)
• How about playing tennis after school?
  (방과 후에 테니스 치는 게 어때?)

P.62~63 LISTEN UP

Ⓐ Listen and circle.

1 G: Do you like to listen to music?
   (너는 음악 듣는 것을 좋아하니?)
   B: No, I don't. I like to read books.
   (아니, 안 좋아해. 나는 책 읽는 것을 좋아해.)

2 G: Does your sister like to take photos?
   (네 여동생은 사진 찍는 것을 좋아하니?)
   B: Yes, she does. She has a good camera.
   (응, 좋아해. 그녀는 좋은 카메라를 가지고 있어.)

3 G: Do they like to do puzzles?
   (그들은 퍼즐 맞추는 것을 좋아하니?)
   B: Yes, they do. They like to do them together.
   (응, 좋아해. 그들은 함께 퍼즐 맞추는 것을 좋아해.)

Ⓑ Listen and check.

1 B: What do you like to do in your free time?
   (너는 여가시간에 무엇을 하는 것을 좋아하니?)
   G: I like to watch movies. What about you?
   (나는 영화 보는 것을 좋아해. 너는?)
   B: Me too. How about going to a movie after
   school? (나도. 방과 후에 영화 보러 가는 게 어때?)
   G: Sure. That sounds good. (그래. 좋아.)

2 G: What do you like to do on weekends?
   (너는 주말에 무엇을 하는 것을 좋아하니?)
   B: I like to go swimming with my father.
   (나는 아빠와 수영하러 가는 것을 좋아해.)
   G: That's great. (멋지다.)

3 B: Do you like to play sports?
   (너는 운동하는 것을 좋아하니?)
   G: Yes, I do. I like to play tennis.

(응, 좋아해. 나는 테니스 치는 것을 좋아해.)

B: Oh, I like tennis, too. How about playing together on Saturday?
(오, 나도 테니스 좋아해. 토요일에 같이 테니스 치는 게 어때?)

G: Sure. (그래.)

4 G: Do you like to play computer games?
(너는 컴퓨터 게임 하는 것을 좋아하니?)

B: No, I don't. What about you?
(아니, 안 좋아해. 너는?)

G: I like to play computer games. They're fun.
(나는 컴퓨터 게임 하는 것을 좋아해. 재미있어.)

C Listen and check.

1 B: Do you like to do puzzles?
(너는 퍼즐 맞추는 것을 좋아하니?)

G: Yes, I do. It's my hobby.
(응, 좋아해. 그게 내 취미야.)

B: Good. How about doing puzzles after school?
(잘됐다. 방과 후에 퍼즐 맞추기 하는 게 어때?)

G: That sounds great! (좋아!)

Question: They will do puzzles after school.
(그들은 방과 후에 퍼즐 맞추기를 할 것이다.)

2 B: What do you like to do in your free time?
(너는 여가시간에 무엇을 하는 것을 좋아하니?)

G: I like to listen to music. What about you?
(나는 음악 듣는 것을 좋아해. 너는?)

B: I like to take photos.
(나는 사진 찍는 것을 좋아해.)

G: Do you have a camera? (너는 카메라가 있니?)

B: Yes, I have a good camera.
(응, 나는 좋은 카메라를 가지고 있어.)

Question: The girl likes to take photos.
(소녀는 사진 찍는 것을 좋아한다.)

D Listen and mark.

1 G: David, what do you like to do in your free time?
(David, 너는 여가시간에 무엇을 하는 것을 좋아하니?)

B: I like to read books. (나는 책 읽는 것을 좋아해.)

G: Do you like to listen to music, too?
(너는 음악 듣는 것도 좋아하니?)

B: Yes, I do. (응, 좋아해.)

2 B: Christine, do you like to do puzzles?
(Christine, 너는 퍼즐 맞추는 것을 좋아하니?)

G: No, I don't. It's boring.

(아니, 안 좋아해. 그건 지루해.)

B: Then, what do you like to do?
(그럼, 너는 무엇을 하는 것을 좋아하니?)

G: I like to take photos.
(나는 사진 찍는 것을 좋아해.)

3 B: Amy, how about playing computer games after school?
(Amy, 방과 후에 컴퓨터 게임 하는 게 어때?)

G: Sure. I like to play computer games. It's my hobby.
(그래. 나는 컴퓨터 게임 하는 것을 좋아해. 그게 내 취미야.)

P.63 ## LET'S SPEAK WITH BUDDY

Listen and say.

Tom: Do you like to go swimming?
(너는 수영하러 가는 것을 좋아하니?)

Jack: No, I don't. I can't swim.
(아니, 안 좋아해. 난 수영 못 해.)

Ann: What do you like to do?
(너는 무엇을 하는 것을 좋아하니?)

Jenny: I like to go swimming.
(나는 수영하러 가는 것을 좋아해.)

Jack: Oh, I like to go swimming, too! It's my favorite hobby.
(오, 나도 수영하러 가는 것을 좋아해! 그게 내가 가장 좋아하는 취미야.)

Jack: Let's go swimming! (수영하러 가자!)

P.64~65 ## DICTATION

A Listen and write the words.

1 play tennis (테니스를 치다)
2 take photos (사진을 찍다)
3 watch movies (영화를 보다)
4 listen to music (음악을 듣다)
5 play computer games (컴퓨터 게임을 하다)

B Listen and write the words.

1 What do you like to do in your free time?
(너는 여가시간에 무엇을 하는 것을 좋아하니?)
2 I like to read books. (나는 책 읽는 것을 좋아해.)
3 How about doing puzzles after school?
(방과 후에 퍼즐 맞추기 하는 게 어때?)
4 Does she like to take photos?

(그녀는 사진 찍는 것을 좋아하니?)
5 I like to go swimming with my father.
   (나는 아빠와 수영하러 가는 것을 좋아해.)

C Listen and fill in the blanks.

1 **G**: David, what do you like to do in your free time?
   (David, 너는 여가시간에 무엇을 하는 것을 좋아하니?)
   B: I like to play sports. (나는 운동하는 것을 좋아해.)
   G: Do you like to play tennis?
   (너는 테니스 치는 것을 좋아하니?)
   B: Yes, I do. (응, 좋아해.)

2 **B**: Do you like to do puzzles?
   (너는 퍼즐 맞추는 것을 좋아하니?)
   G: Yes, I do. It's my hobby.
   (응, 좋아해. 그게 내 취미야.)
   B: Good. How about doing puzzles after school?
   (잘됐다. 방과 후에 퍼즐 맞추기 하는 게 어때?)
   G: That sounds great! (좋아!)

3 **B**: What do you like to do in your free time?
   (너는 여가시간에 무엇을 하는 것을 좋아하니?)
   G: I like to watch movies. What about you?
   (나는 영화 보는 것을 좋아해. 너는?)
   B: Me too. How about going to a movie after school? (나도. 방과 후에 영화 보러 가는 게 어때?)
   G: Sure. That sounds good. (그래. 좋아.)

P.66~67 ### UNIT TEST

1 ⓐ listen to music (음악을 듣다)
   ⓑ watch movies (영화를 보다)
   ⓒ take photos (사진을 찍다)
   ⓓ play computer games (컴퓨터 게임을 하다)

2 ⓐ He likes to do puzzles.
   (그는 퍼즐 맞추는 것을 좋아한다.)
   ⓑ He likes to listen to music.
   (그는 음악 듣는 것을 좋아한다.)
   ⓒ She likes to read books.
   (그녀는 책 읽는 것을 좋아한다.)
   ⓓ She likes to watch movies.
   (그녀는 영화 보는 것을 좋아한다.)

3 **B**: Do you like to go swimming?
   (너는 수영하러 가는 것을 좋아하니?)
   G: No, I don't. I can't swim. I like to play tennis.
   (아니, 안 좋아해. 나는 수영 못 해. 나는 테니스 치는 것

을 좋아해.)

4 ⓐ **B**: What do you like to do in your free time?
   (너는 여가시간에 무엇을 하는 것을 좋아하니?)
   G: I like to play computer games.
   (나는 컴퓨터 게임 하는 것을 좋아해.)
   ⓑ **B**: How about going to a movie?
   (영화 보러 가는 게 어때?)
   G: Sure. I like to watch movies.
   (그래. 나는 영화 보는 것을 좋아해.)
   ⓒ **B**: Do you like to listen to music?
   (너는 음악 듣는 것을 좋아하니?)
   G: Yes, I do. It's my hobby.
   (응, 좋아해. 그게 내 취미야.)
   ⓓ **B**: Do you like to do puzzles?
   (너는 퍼즐 맞추는 것을 좋아하니?)
   G: No, I don't. It's boring.
   (아니, 안 좋아해. 그건 지루해.)

5 **B**: Do you like to read books?
   (너는 책 읽는 것을 좋아하니?)
   G: No, I don't. (아니, 안 좋아해.)
   B: Then, what do you like to do?
   (그럼, 너는 무엇을 하는 것을 좋아하니?)
   G: _____
   ⓐ No, I don't. (아니.)
   ⓑ Sure. That sounds good. (그래. 좋은 생각이야.)
   ⓒ I like to listen to music.
   (나는 음악 듣는 것을 좋아해.)
   ⓓ How about playing computer games?
   (컴퓨터 게임 하는 게 어때?)

6 ⓐ **G**: What do you like to do on weekends?
   (너는 주말에 무엇을 하는 것을 좋아하니?)
   B: I like to go swimming with my father.
   (나는 아빠와 수영하러 가는 것을 좋아해.)
   ⓑ **G**: Does he like to take photos?
   (그는 사진 찍는 것을 좋아하니?)
   B: Yes, he does. (응, 좋아해.)
   ⓒ **G**: How about listening to music?
   (음악 듣는 게 어때?)
   B: That sounds good. (좋은 생각이야.)
   ⓓ **G**: What do you like to do in your free time?
   (너는 여가시간에 무엇을 하는 것을 좋아하니?)
   B: No, I don't like to watch movies.
   (아니, 나는 영화 보는 것을 좋아하지 않아.)

7 **G**: Do you like to play computer games?
   (너는 컴퓨터 게임 하는 것을 좋아하니?)
   B: No, I don't. (아니, 안 좋아해.)
   G: Then, what do you like to do?
   (그럼, 너는 무엇을 하는 것을 좋아하니?)

B: I like to do puzzles. How about doing puzzles after school?
(나는 퍼즐 맞추는 것을 좋아해. 방과 후에 퍼즐 맞추기 하는 게 어때?)

G: Sure. That sounds good. (그래. 좋아.)

Question: What will they do?
(그들은 무엇을 할 것인가?)

8 B: Lisa, how about playing tennis after school?
(Lisa, 방과 후에 테니스 치는 게 어때?)

G: No, I don't like to play sports.
(싫어, 나는 운동하는 것을 안 좋아해.)

B: Then, what do you like to do?
(그럼, 너는 무엇을 하는 것을 좋아하니?)

G: I like to take photos. (나는 사진 찍는 것을 좋아해.)

B: Do you have a camera? (너는 카메라가 있니?)

G: Yes. I have a good camera.
(응. 나는 좋은 카메라를 가지고 있어.)

Question: The girl likes to take photos.
(소녀는 사진 찍는 것을 좋아한다.)

UNIT 8 AT THE FESTIVAL

ANSWERS

P.68

P.69

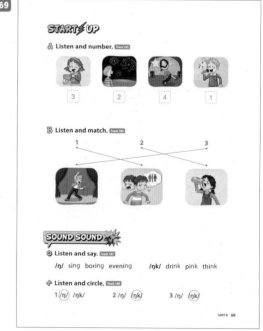

P.70

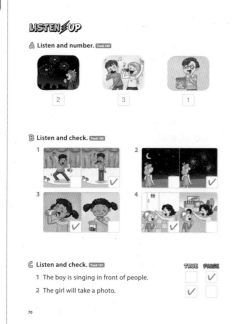

C
1 doing, fireworks
2 looking, for, restroom
3 fun, cool, dancing, photo

P.74~75 **UNIT TEST**

1 ⓒ 2 ⓓ 3 ⓐ 4 ⓑ
5 ⓒ 6 ⓓ 7 ⓑ 8 ⓒ

SCRIPTS & 해석

P.68 **ARE YOU READY?**

⚡ **Listen and number.**

1 G: What are they doing?
  (그들은 무엇을 하고 있는 거야?)
  B: They are dancing on the stage.
  (그들은 무대 위에서 춤추고 있어.)

2 W: Are you eating snacks? (너 간식 먹고 있니?)
  B: Yes, I am. Can I drink some soda?
   (네, 먹고 있어요. 탄산음료 좀 마셔도 돼요?)
  W: Yes, you can. (그럼, 마시렴.)

3 M: Can I help you? (도와줄까?)
  G: Yes, please. I'm looking for a restroom.
   (네. 저는 화장실을 찾고 있어요.)
  M: There is a restroom over there.
   (저기에 화장실이 있단다.)

⭐ **Listen and repeat.**

sing (노래하다)
dance on a stage (무대 위에서 춤추다)
look for a restroom (화장실을 찾다)
eat snacks (간식을 먹다)
drink soda (탄산음료를 마시다)
watch the fireworks (불꽃놀이를 보다)

P.72~73 **DICTATION**

A
1 snacks   2 drink   3 stage
4 watch   5 restroom

B
1 doing   2 eating   3 soda
4 Can   5 singing

P.69 **START UP**

A **Listen and number.**

1 sing (노래하다)
2 watch the fireworks (불꽃놀이를 보다)
3 eat snacks (간식을 먹다)
4 dance on a stage (무대 위에서 춤추다)

B **Listen and match.**

1 G: What are you doing? (너는 무엇을 하고 있니?)
  B: I'm looking for a restroom.

(나는 화장실을 찾고 있어.)

2 G: Is she drinking soda?
(그녀는 탄산음료를 마시고 있니?)
B: No, she isn't. She's drinking water.
(아니, 그렇지 않아. 그녀는 물을 마시고 있어.)

3 B: Can I dance on the stage?
(무대 위에서 춤춰도 돼요?)
W: Sure. Go ahead. (그럼. 그렇게 하렴.)

P.69 ## SOUND SOUND

🔷 Listen and say.

/ŋ/ sing (노래하다)   boring (지루한)
evening (저녁)
/ŋk/ drink (마시다)   pink (분홍색의)
think (생각하다)

➕ Listen and circle.

1 evening   **2** drink   **3** think

P.70~71 ## LISTEN UP

Ⓐ Listen and number.

1 G: What is he doing? (그는 무엇을 하고 있니?)
B: He's eating snacks. (그는 간식을 먹고 있어.)
G: Oh, I want some snacks, too.
(오, 나도 간식 먹고 싶어.)

2 G: What is she doing? (그녀는 무엇을 하고 있니?)
B: She is watching the fireworks.
(그녀는 불꽃놀이를 보고 있어.)
G: Cool! Let's join her. (멋지다! 그녀와 같이 보자.)

3 G: What are they doing?
(그들은 무엇을 하고 있니?)
B: They are dancing and singing.
(그들은 춤추며 노래하고 있어.)
G: They're so cute. (정말 귀엽다.)

Ⓑ Listen and check.

1 M: Where is he? (그는 어디에 있니?)
G: He's on the stage. (무대 위에 있어요.)
M: What is he doing there?
(거기서 무엇을 하고 있는 거니?)
G: He's singing. (노래하고 있어요.)

2 B: Hey, what are you doing?
(얘, 너 무엇을 하고 있니?)

G: I'm watching the fireworks. Aren't they
pretty? (불꽃놀이를 보고 있어. 예쁘지 않니?)
B: Wow, cool! I want to take a photo.
(와, 멋지다! 사진 찍고 싶어.)
G: Good idea. (좋은 생각이야.)

3 G: Can I drink some soda?
(탄산음료 좀 마셔도 돼요?)
M: Sure. Go ahead. Do you want some snacks,
too? (그럼. 그렇게 하렴. 간식도 좀 먹겠니?)
G: No, thank you. (아뇨, 괜찮아요.)
M: Okay. (그래.)

4 B: Can you help me, please? (좀 도와주실래요?)
W: Sure. What's the matter?
(물론이지. 무슨 일이니?)
B: I'm looking for a restroom.
(저는 화장실을 찾고 있어요.)
W: Oh, it's over there. (오, 저기에 있단다.)

Ⓒ Listen and check.

1 G: There are a lot of people. Let's go over
there. (사람들이 많이 있네. 저기에 가 보자.)
B: What are they doing?
(그들은 무엇을 하고 있는 거야?)
G: They are singing. (노래하고 있어.)
B: They are singing very well.
(노래를 아주 잘하는구나.)

Question: The boy is singing in front of
people.
(소년은 사람들 앞에서 노래하고 있다.)

2 G: Dad, this festival is a lot of fun.
(아빠, 이 축제는 정말 재미있네요.)
M: Yeah, it's cool! (그래, 멋지구나!)
G: Look over there. Is he dancing on the
stage?
(저기 좀 보세요. 그는 무대 위에서 춤추고 있는 건가
요?)
M: Yes, he is. (그래, 그렇구나.)
G: Can I take a photo? (사진 찍어도 돼요?)
M: Sure. Go ahead. (그럼. 그렇게 하렴.)

Question: The girl will take a photo.
(소녀는 사진을 찍을 것이다.)

Ⓓ Listen and write.

1 G: What is Ben doing? (Ben은 무엇을 하고 있니?)
B: He's watching the fireworks.
(그는 불꽃놀이를 보고 있어.)
G: Cool! Let's join him. (멋지다! 그와 같이 보자.)

2 G: What is Lily doing? (Lily는 무엇을 하고 있니?)
  B: She is singing on the stage.
    (그녀는 무대 위에서 노래하고 있어.)
  G: She's singing very well.
    (그녀는 노래를 아주 잘하는구나.)

3 G: I'm looking for Mike. Where is he?
    (나는 Mike를 찾고 있어. 그는 어디에 있니?)
  B: He's at the food truck. (그는 푸드 트럭에 있어.)
  G: Is he eating snacks? (그는 간식을 먹고 있니?)
  B: No, he isn't. He's drinking soda.
    (아니, 그렇지 않아. 그는 탄산음료를 마시고 있어.)

P.71 LET'S SPEAK WITH BUDDY

◉ Listen and say.

Jenny: Look! The boys are dancing on the stage.
    (저기 좀 봐! 소년들이 무대 위에서 춤추고 있어.)
Jack: Let's go over there. (저기에 가 보자.)

Jenny: Wow, cool! (와, 멋지다!)

Jack: Can I dance on the stage?
    (무대 위에서 춤춰도 돼요?)
Staff: Sure. Go ahead. (물론이지. 그렇게 하렴.)

Ann: What is he doing? (그는 무엇을 하고 있는 거니?)
Tom: Is he dancing? (춤추고 있는 거야?)

P.72~73 DICTATION

A Listen and write the words.

1 eat snacks (간식을 먹다)
2 drink soda (탄산음료를 마시다)
3 dance on a stage (무대 위에서 춤추다)
4 watch the fireworks (불꽃놀이를 보다)
5 look for a restroom (화장실을 찾다)

B Listen and write the words.

1 What are they doing? (그들은 무엇을 하고 있니?)
2 Are you eating snacks? (너 간식 먹고 있니?)
3 He is drinking soda.
  (그는 탄산음료를 마시고 있어.)
4 Can I take a photo? (사진 찍어도 돼요?)
5 She is singing very well.
  (그녀는 노래를 아주 잘하는구나.)

C Listen and fill in the blanks.

1 **G**: What is she doing? (그녀는 무엇을 하고 있니?)
  B: She is watching the fireworks.

    (그녀는 불꽃놀이를 보고 있어.)
  G: Cool! Let's join her. (멋지다! 그녀와 같이 보자.)

2 M: Can I help you? (도와줄까?)
  G: Yes, please. I'm looking for a restroom.
    (네. 저는 화장실을 찾고 있어요.)
  M: There is a restroom over there.
    (저기에 화장실이 있단다.)

3 G: Dad, this festival is a lot of fun.
    (아빠, 이 축제는 정말 재미있네요.)
  M: Yeah, it's cool! (그래, 멋지구나!)
  G: Look over there. Is he dancing on the
    stage?
    (저기 좀 보세요. 그는 무대 위에서 춤추고 있는 건가
    요?)
  M: Yes, he is. (그래, 그렇구나.)
  G: Can I take a photo? (사진 찍어도 돼요?)
  M: Sure. Go ahead. (그럼. 그렇게 하렴.)

P.74~75 UNIT TEST

1 ⓐ drink soda (탄산음료를 마시다)
  ⓑ dance on a stage (무대 위에서 춤추다)
  ⓒ watch the fireworks (불꽃놀이를 보다)
  ⓓ look for a restroom (화장실을 찾다)

2 ⓐ She is singing. (그녀는 노래하고 있다.)
  ⓑ She is eating ice cream.
    (그녀는 아이스크림을 먹고 있다.)
  ⓒ He is drinking soda. (그는 탄산음료를 마시고 있다.)
  ⓓ He is eating snacks. (그는 간식을 먹고 있다.)

3 **B**: Is she singing on the stage?
    (그녀는 무대 위에서 노래하고 있니?)
  G: No, she isn't. She's dancing.
    (아니, 그렇지 않아. 그녀는 춤추고 있어.)

4 ⓐ **G**: What are you doing? (너는 무엇을 하고 있니?)
  B: I'm looking for the stage.
    (나는 무대를 찾고 있어.)
  ⓑ **G**: Can I help you? (도와줄까?)
  B: Yes, please. I'm looking for a restroom.
    (응. 나는 화장실을 찾고 있어.)
  ⓒ **G**: Are you watching the fireworks?
    (너는 불꽃놀이를 보고 있니?)
  B: Yes, I am. (응, 그래.)
  ⓓ **G**: Can I take a photo? (사진 찍어도 되니?)
  B: Sure. Go ahead. (물론이지. 그렇게 해.)

5 **B**: There are a lot of people. Let's go over there.
    (사람들이 많이 있네. 저기에 가 보자.)

G: What are they doing? Are they dancing on the stage?
(그들은 무엇을 하고 있는 거야? 무대 위에서 춤추고 있는 거야?)

B: _____

ⓐ No, you can't. (아니, 안 돼.)

ⓑ No, I'm singing. (아니, 나는 노래하고 있어.)

ⓒ Yes, they are dancing very well.
(응, 그들은 춤을 아주 잘 추는구나.)

ⓓ Yes, they are watching the fireworks.
(응, 그들은 불꽃놀이를 보고 있어.)

6 ⓐ **B**: What is he doing? (그는 무엇을 하고 있니?)
　　G: He is drinking soda.
　　　　(그는 탄산음료를 마시고 있어.)

　ⓑ **B**: Are you watching the fireworks?
　　　　(너는 불꽃놀이를 보고 있니?)
　　G: No, I'm not. (아니, 그렇지 않아.)

　ⓒ **B**: Can I sing on the stage?
　　　　(무대 위에서 노래해도 돼요?)
　　W: Sure. Go ahead. (물론이지. 그렇게 하렴.)

　ⓓ **B**: Can you help me? (좀 도와줄래?)
　　G: Yes, please. I'm looking for a restroom.
　　　　(응. 나는 화장실을 찾고 있어.)

7 **B**: Hey, what are you doing?
　　　(얘, 너 무엇을 하고 있니?)

　G: I'm watching the fireworks. Aren't they pretty?
　　　(불꽃놀이를 보고 있어. 예쁘지 않니?)

　B: Wow, cool! I want to take a photo.
　　　(와, 멋지다! 사진 찍고 싶어.)

　G: Good idea. (좋은 생각이야.)

　Question: What is the girl doing?
　　　　　(소녀는 무엇을 하고 있는가?)

8 **G**: This festival is a lot of fun.
　　　(이 축제는 정말 재미있구나.)

　B: Yeah, it's cool! Look over there. My sister is on the stage.
　　　(응, 멋져! 저기 좀 봐. 내 여동생이 무대 위에 있어.)

　G: What is she doing there? Is she singing?
　　　(그녀는 저기서 무엇을 하고 있는 거야? 노래하고 있는 거니?)

　B: Yes, she is. (응, 그래.)

　G: Wow, she is singing very well.
　　　(와, 그녀는 노래를 아주 잘하는구나.)

　Question: Who is singing on the stage?
　　　　　(누가 무대 위에서 노래하고 있는가?)

ANSWERS

P.76

P.77

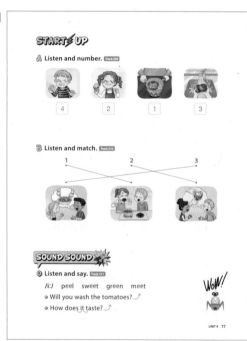

P.78

LISTEN UP

A Listen and match. Track 212

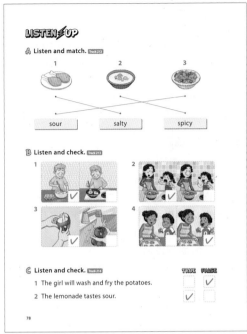

1   2   3

sour   salty   spicy

B Listen and check. Track 213

1 ✓   2 ✓

3 ✓   4 ✓

C Listen and check. Track 214

	TRUE	FALSE
1 The girl will wash and fry the potatoes.		✓
2 The lemonade tastes sour.	✓	

78

P.79

D Listen and number in order. Track 215

1   2   3

2 → 1 → 3

LET'S SPEAK WITH BUDDY

Listen and say. Track 216

What are you doing?

Will you mix the eggs and sugar, please?

Okay.

I'm making cookies.

30 minutes later

It's too salty!

SALT

It smells delicious! Can I try one?

Sure. How does it taste?

Oh, no! That was salt, not sugar.

↻ Listen again and repeat.

UNIT 9   79

P.80~81 DICTATION

A 1 x   2 o, u   3 i
   4 s, h   5 e, e

B 1 salty   2 fry   3 taste
   4 try   5 sour

C 1 try, How, spicy
   2 making, Will, mix
   3 pizza, help, wash, peel

P.82~83 UNIT TEST

1 ⓑ   2 ⓒ   3 ⓐ   4 ⓓ
5 ⓒ   6 ⓓ   7 ⓐ   8 ⓑ

SCRIPTS & 해석

P.76 ARE YOU READY?

⚡ **Listen and number.**

1 **W**: Will you wash the tomatoes?
   (토마토 좀 씻어주겠니?)
   B: Okay. (네.)

2 **W**: How does it taste? (맛이 어떠니?)
   B: It's very salty. (너무 짜요.)

★ **Listen and repeat.**

wash (씻다)   peel (껍질을 벗기다)
mix (섞다)   fry (튀기다)
sweet (달콤한)   salty (짠)
sour (신)   spicy (매운)

P.77 START UP

A Listen and number.

1 fry (튀기다)
2 sweet (달콤한)
3 wash (씻다)
4 sour (신)

B Listen and match.

1 **B**: How does it taste? (맛이 어떠니?)
   G: It tastes spicy. (매워.)

2 **B**: Will you peel the apple, please?
   (사과 좀 깎아줄래?)
   G: Sure. (응.)

3 **B**: Will you mix the salad, please?
   (샐러드 좀 섞어줄래?)
   G: Okay, I will. (응, 그럴게.)

37

SOUND SOUND

🔊 **Listen and say.**

/iː/ peel (껍질을 벗기다)   sweet (달콤한)
    green (초록색의)   meet (만나다)

○ Will you wash the tomatoes?
  (토마토 좀 씻어주겠니?)
○ How does it taste? (맛이 어떠니?)

LISTEN UP

Ⓐ **Listen and match.**

1 B: Can I try the chicken? (닭고기 먹어봐도 되니?)
  G: Sure. How does it taste? (그럼. 맛이 어떠니?)
  B: It's salty. (짜.)

2 G: Do you want to try the soup?
    (수프 좀 먹어볼래?)
  B: Yes. (응.)
  G: How does it taste? (맛이 어떠니?)
  B: It's spicy. (매워.)

3 B: Can I try the salad? (샐러드 먹어봐도 되니?)
  G: Yes. How does it taste? (응. 맛이 어떠니?)
  B: It tastes sour. (셔.)

Ⓑ **Listen and check.**

1 M: Are you making dinner? (저녁 만들고 있어요?)
  W: Yes, I am. Can you help me?
    (네. 좀 도와줄래요?)
  M: Sure. What should I do?
    (물론이죠. 뭘 하면 되죠?)
  W: Will you mix the eggs, please?
    (계란 좀 섞어줄래요?)
  M: Okay, I will. (네, 그럴게요.)

2 G: Mom, can I try this soup?
    (엄마, 이 수프 먹어봐도 돼요?)
  W: Sure. How does it taste? (그럼. 맛이 어떠니?)
  G: It's too spicy. (너무 매워요.)
  W: Oh, will you bring me some water?
    (오, 물 좀 가져다주겠니?)
  G: Sure. (네.)

3 B: You look busy. What are you doing?
    (너 바빠 보인다. 뭐 하고 있니?)
  G: I'm making salad. (샐러드를 만들고 있어.)
  B: Oh, I'll help you. (오, 내가 도와줄게.)
  G: Thank you. Will you peel the apple, please?
    (고마워. 사과 좀 깎아줄래?)
  B: Sure. (그래.)

4 B: Something smells delicious, Mom!
    (엄마, 맛있는 냄새가 나요!)
  W: I'm making cookies. Do you want to try
    one? (쿠키를 만들고 있단다. 하나 먹어볼래?)
  B: Yes, I do! (네, 먹을래요!)
  W: How does it taste? (맛이 어떠니?)
  B: It's sweet and delicious. (달콤하고 맛있어요.)

Ⓒ **Listen and check.**

1 G: Dad, are you making lunch?
    (아빠, 점심 만들고 계세요?)
  M: Yes. I'm making pizza. Can you help me?
    (그래. 피자를 만들고 있단다. 좀 도와주겠니?)
  G: Sure. What should I do?
    (물론이죠. 뭘 하면 돼요?)
  M: Will you wash and peel the potatoes?
    (감자를 씻어서 껍질 좀 벗겨주겠니?)
  G: Okay. (네.)

  Question: The girl will wash and fry the
          potatoes.
          (소녀는 감자를 씻어서 튀길 것이다.)

2 G: You look busy. What are you doing?
    (너 바빠 보인다. 뭐 하고 있니?)
  B: I'm making lemonade.
    (레모네이드를 만들고 있어.)
  G: Can I try some? (좀 먹어봐도 되니?)
  B: Sure. How does it taste? (그럼. 맛이 어떠니?)
  G: It's too sour. How about adding some
    sugar? (너무 셔. 설탕을 좀 넣는 게 어때?)
  B: That's a good idea. (좋은 생각이야.)

  Question: The lemonade tastes sour.
          (레모네이드는 시다.)

Ⓓ **Listen and number in order.**

B: Mom, something smells delicious.
  (엄마, 맛있는 냄새가 나요.)
W: I'm frying onion rings and making potato
  soup. (어니언링을 튀기고 감자 수프를 만들고 있단다.)
B: Can I try an onion ring?
  (어니언링 하나 먹어봐도 돼요?)
W: Sure. Try this one. (*pause*) How does it taste?
  (그럼. 이거 먹어 보렴. 맛이 어떠니?)
B: It tastes delicious. (맛있어요.)
W: Do you want to try the potato soup, too?
  (감자 수프도 먹어볼래?)
B: Yes, please. (*pause*) Oh, the soup is a little
  salty. (네, 주세요. 오, 수프는 좀 짜요.)
W: Then, let's add one more potato. Will you
  peel it? (그럼, 감자를 하나 더 넣자. 감자 껍질 좀 벗겨주겠니?)

B: Okay, Mom. (네, 엄마.)

P.79 LET'S SPEAK WITH BUDDY

🔊 Listen and say.

Jenny: What are you doing? (뭐 하고 있니?)
Jack: I'm making cookies. (쿠키를 만들고 있어.)

Jack: Will you mix the eggs and sugar, please?
　　　(계란과 설탕 좀 섞어줄래?)
Jenny: Okay. (그래.)

30 minutes later (30분 후)
Jenny: It smells delicious! Can I try one?
　　　(맛있는 냄새가 나! 하나 먹어봐도 돼?)
Jack: Sure. How does it taste? (그럼. 맛이 어떠니?)

Jenny: It's too salty! (너무 짜!)
Jack: Oh, no! That was salt, not sugar.
　　　(오, 이런! 그건 설탕이 아니라 소금이었어.)

P.80~81 DICTATION

A Listen and write the letters.

1 mix (섞다)
2 sour (신)
3 spicy (매운)
4 wash (씻다)
5 sweet (달콤한)

B Listen and write the words.

1 The chicken is salty. (그 닭고기는 짜.)
2 Will you fry the onions, please?
　(양파 좀 튀겨줄래?)
3 How does it taste? (그것은 맛이 어떠니?)
4 Can I try this soup? (이 수프 먹어봐도 되니?)
5 The lemonade tastes too sour.
　(그 레모네이드는 너무 셔.)

C Listen and fill in the blanks.

1 G: Do you want to try the soup?
　　(수프 좀 먹어볼래?)
　B: Yes. (응.)
　G: How does it taste? (맛이 어떠니?)
　B: It's spicy. (매워.)

2 B: You look busy. What are you doing?
　　(너 바빠 보인다. 뭐 하고 있니?)
　G: I'm making dinner. (저녁 만들고 있어.)

B: Oh, I'll help you. (오, 내가 도와줄게.)
G: Thank you. Will you mix the salad, please?
　(고마워. 샐러드 좀 섞어줄래?)
B: Sure. (그래.)

3 G: Dad, are you making lunch?
　　(아빠, 점심 만들고 계세요?)
　M: Yes. I'm making pizza. Can you help me?
　　(그래. 피자를 만들고 있단다. 좀 도와주겠니?)
　G: Sure. What should I do?
　　(물론이죠. 뭘 하면 돼요?)
　M: Will you wash and peel the potatoes?
　　(감자를 씻어서 껍질 좀 벗겨주겠니?)
　G: Okay. (네.)

P.82~83 UNIT TEST

1 ⓐ salty (짠)
　ⓑ sweet (달콤한)
　ⓒ sour (신)
　ⓓ spicy (매운)

2 ⓐ She is frying the eggs. (그녀는 계란을 부치고 있다.)
　ⓑ He is peeling the eggs.
　　(그는 계란 껍질을 벗기고 있다.)
　ⓒ She is mixing the eggs. (그녀는 계란을 섞고 있다.)
　ⓓ He is washing the eggs. (그는 계란을 씻고 있다.)

3 B: Can I try the chicken? (닭고기 먹어봐도 되니?)
　G: Sure. How does it taste? (그럼. 맛이 어떠니?)
　B: It's too spicy. (너무 매워.)

4 W: What will the boy say to the girl?
　　(소년이 소녀에게 할 말은 무엇인가?)
　ⓐ Will you wash the potatoes, please?
　　(감자 좀 씻어줄래?)
　ⓑ Will you peel the tomatoes, please?
　　(토마토 껍질 좀 벗겨줄래?)
　ⓒ Will you fry the potatoes, please?
　　(감자 좀 튀겨줄래?)
　ⓓ Will you wash the tomatoes, please?
　　(토마토 좀 씻어줄래?)

5 B: Do you want to try the lemonade?
　　(레모네이드 좀 마셔볼래?)
　G: Yes. (응.)
　B: How does it taste? (맛이 어떠니?)
　G: ＿＿＿＿＿＿＿＿＿＿＿＿＿
　ⓐ I'm making lemonade.
　　(난 레모네이드를 만들고 있어.)
　ⓑ What should I do? (뭘 하면 되니?)

ⓒ It's too sour. (너무 셔.)

ⓓ Can I try some? (좀 마셔봐도 되니?)

6 ⓐ **G**: Will you peel the apple, please?
  (사과 좀 깎아줄래?)

  B: Okay, I will. (응, 그럴게.)

ⓑ **G**: Do you want to try a cookie?
  (쿠키 좀 먹어볼래?)

  B: Yes, I do. (응, 먹을래.)

ⓒ **G**: How does it taste? (맛이 어떠니?)

  B: It tastes sweet. (달콤해.)

ⓓ **G**: Can you help me? (좀 도와주겠니?)

  B: Sure. Will you wash the potatoes?
  (물론이지. 감자 좀 씻어줄래?)

7 **M**: Something smells delicious!
  (맛있는 냄새가 나네요!)

  W: Yes. I'm making lunch. Can you help me?
  (네. 점심 만들고 있어요. 좀 도와줄래요?)

  M: Sure. What should I do? (물론이죠. 뭘 하면 되죠?)

  W: Will you fry the onions, please?
  (양파 좀 튀겨줄래요?)

  M: Okay. (네.)

  Question: What will the man do next?
  (남자가 다음에 할 일은 무엇인가?)

8 **B**: You look busy. What are you doing?
  (너 바빠 보인다. 뭐 하고 있니?)

  G: I'm making soup. (수프를 만들고 있어.)

  B: Can I try some? (좀 먹어봐도 되니?)

  G: Sure. How does it taste? (그럼. 맛이 어떠니?)

  B: It's delicious, but a little salty. How about
  adding some water?
  (맛있지만 조금 짜. 물을 좀 넣는 게 어때?)

  G: That's a good idea. (좋은 생각이야.)

  Question: How does the soup taste?
  (수프의 맛은 어떠한가?)

ANSWERS

P.84

P.85

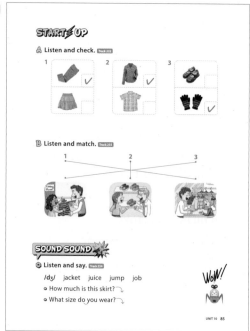

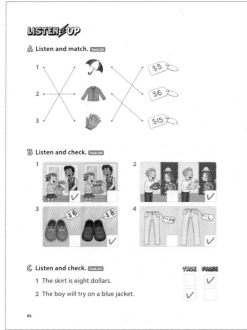

LISTEN UP

A Listen and match. Track 236

1, 2, 3 → umbrella, jacket, gloves → $5, $6, $15

B Listen and check. Track 236

1 ✓
2 ✓
3 $6 / $8 → ✓
4 M / L → ✓

C Listen and check. Track 237

	TRUE	FALSE
1 The skirt is eight dollars.		✓
2 The boy will try on a blue jacket.	✓	

86

D Listen and write. Track 238

ⓐ $6 ⓑ $8 ⓒ $8 ⓓ $9

1 I'll take … ⓓ
2 I'll take … ⓑ

LET'S SPEAK WITH BUDDY

Listen and say. Track 239

I like that jacket. How about that one, Jenny?

Excuse me. How much is this jacket?

It's fifteen dollars.

Cool. I like it, too.

Can I try it on?

Sure.

I'll take it.

↻ Listen again and repeat.

UNIT 10 87

DICTATION

A
1 i   2 v   3 o, e
4 j, a   5 r, e

B
1 take   2 try   3 shirt
4 wear   5 pants

C
1 help, gloves
2 How, much, take, it, size
3 jacket, blue, try, on

UNIT TEST

1 ⓒ   2 ⓒ   3 ⓑ   4 ⓒ
5 ⓓ   6 ⓑ   7 ⓒ   8 ⓐ

SCRIPTS & 해석

ARE YOU READY?

⚡ **Listen and number.**

1 **M:** May I help you? (도와드릴까요?)
B: Yes, please. I'm looking for an umbrella.
(네. 우산을 찾고 있어요.)

2 **G:** How much is this skirt? (이 치마 얼마예요?)
W: It's twelve dollars. (12달러입니다.)

3 **W:** What size do you wear?
(사이즈가 어떻게 되세요?)
B: I wear a small. (작은 사이즈를 입어요.)

⭐ **Listen and repeat.**

shirt (셔츠)   jacket (재킷)   skirt (치마)
pants (바지)   shoes (구두)   gloves (장갑)
umbrella (우산)

START UP

A Listen and check.

1 pants (바지)
2 jacket (새킷)
3 gloves (장갑)

B Listen and match.

1 **M:** May I help you? (도와드릴까요?)
G: Yes. I'm looking for a shirt.
(네. 셔츠를 찾고 있어요.)

2 **G:** How much are these shoes?
(이 구두 얼마예요?)
M: They're ten dollars. (10달러입니다.)

3 **G:** Can I try on this skirt?
(이 치마 입어봐도 될까요?)
M: Sure. What size do you wear?

41

(그럼요. 사이즈가 어떻게 되세요?)
G: Medium. (중간 사이즈예요.)

🎧 **Listen and say.**

/dʒ/ jacket (재킷)   juice (주스)
jump (뛰다)   job (직업)

○ How much is this skirt? (이 치마 얼마예요?)
○ What size do you wear? (사이즈가 어떻게 되세요?)

Ⓐ **Listen and match.**

1 W: May I help you? (도와드릴까요?)
B: Yes, please. How much are these gloves?
(네. 이 장갑 얼마예요?)
W: They are five dollars. (5달러입니다.)

2 G: How much is this jacket? (이 재킷 얼마예요?)
M: It's fifteen dollars. (15달러입니다.)
G: I'll take it. (이걸로 할게요.)

3 B: I'm looking for an umbrella.
(저는 우산을 찾고 있어요.)
W: How about this one? It's on sale. It's six
dollars.
(이거 어떠세요? 할인 판매 중이에요. 6달러입니다.)
B: I like it. (마음에 들어요.)

Ⓑ **Listen and check.**

1 M: May I help you? (도와드릴까요?)
G: Yes, please. How much is this shirt?
(네. 이 셔츠 얼마예요?)
M: It's twelve dollars. (12달러입니다.)
G: Good. I'll take it. (좋아요. 이걸로 할게요.)

2 W: Excuse me. I'm looking for a hat.
(실례합니다. 저는 모자를 찾고 있어요.)
M: What about this yellow hat?
(이 노란색 모자 어떠세요?)
W: Oh, I like it. Can I try it on?
(오, 마음에 들어요. 써봐도 될까요?)
M: Sure. Go ahead. (그럼요. 그렇게 하세요.)

3 B: Mom, I like these shoes.
(엄마, 저 이 구두가 마음에 들어요.)
W: They look nice. How much are they?
(멋지구나. 이거 얼마죠?)
M: They're eight dollars. (8달러입니다.)

W: Let's buy them. (이걸 사자.)

4 G: Excuse me. Can I try on these pants?
(실례합니다. 이 바지 입어봐도 될까요?)
W: Sure. What size do you wear?
(그럼요. 사이즈가 어떻게 되세요?)
G: I wear a large. (큰 사이즈를 입어요.)
W: Here they are. (여기 있어요.)

Ⓒ **Listen and check.**

1 G: Excuse me. How much is this skirt?
(실례합니다. 이 치마 얼마예요?)
M: It's ten dollars. (10달러입니다.)
G: How about these pants? (이 바지는요?)
M: They're on sale. They're eight dollars.
(그건 할인 판매 중이에요. 8달러입니다.)
G: Good. I'll take them. (좋네요. 이걸로 할게요.)

Question: The skirt is eight dollars.
(치마는 8달러이다.)

2 W: May I help you? (도와드릴까요?)
B: Yes, please. I'm looking for a jacket.
(네. 재킷을 찾고 있어요.)
W: What about this blue jacket?
(이 파란색 재킷 어떠세요?)
B: I like it. Can I try it on?
(마음에 들어요. 입어봐도 될까요?)
W: Sure. What size do you wear?
(그럼요. 사이즈가 어떻게 되세요?)
B: I wear a medium. (중간 사이즈를 입어요.)

Question: The boy will try on a blue jacket.
(소년은 파란색 재킷을 입어볼 것이다.)

Ⓓ **Listen and write.**

1 B: I like this shirt. How about this one, Mom?
(이 셔츠 마음에 들어요. 이거 어때요, 엄마?)
W: Fine. I like it, too. (좋구나. 나도 마음에 든단다.)
B: Then I'll take it. How much is it?
(그럼 이걸로 할게요. 이거 얼마예요?)
M: It's nine dollars. (9달러입니다.)

2 G: Excuse me. How much is this shirt?
(실례합니다. 이 셔츠 얼마예요?)
M: It's eight dollars. (8달러입니다.)
G: Good. I'll take it. (좋아요. 이걸로 할게요.)
M: What size do you wear?
(사이즈가 어떻게 되세요?)
G: I wear a small. (작은 사이즈를 입어요.)

LET'S SPEAK WITH BUDDY

🎧 **Listen and say.**

Jack: I like that jacket. How about that one, Jenny?
(저 재킷이 마음에 들어. 저거 어때, Jenny?)

Jenny: Cool. I like it, too. (멋지다. 나도 마음에 들어.)

Jack: Excuse me. How much is this jacket?
(실례합니다. 이 재킷 얼마예요?)

Clerk: It's fifteen dollars. (15달러입니다.)

Jack: Can I try it on? (이거 입어봐도 될까요?)

Clerk: Sure. (그럼요.)

Jack: I'll take it. (이걸로 할게요.)

P.88~89 **DICTATION**

Ⓐ **Listen and write the letters.**

1 skirt (치마)
2 gloves (장갑)
3 shoes (구두)
4 jacket (재킷)
5 umbrella (우산)

Ⓑ **Listen and write the words.**

1 I like it. I'll take it.
(이거 마음에 들어요. 이걸로 할게요.)
2 Can I try it on? (이거 입어봐도 될까요?)
3 I'm looking for a shirt. (저는 셔츠를 찾고 있어요.)
4 What size do you wear? (사이즈가 어떻게 되세요?)
5 How much are these pants? (이 바지 얼마예요?)

Ⓒ **Listen and fill in the blanks.**

1 W: May I help you? (도와드릴까요?)
B: Yes, please. How much are these gloves?
(네. 이 장갑 얼마예요?)
W: They are five dollars. (5달러입니다.)

2 G: Excuse me. How much is this shirt?
(실례합니다. 이 셔츠 얼마예요?)
M: It's eight dollars. (8달러입니다.)
G: Good. I'll take it. (좋아요. 이걸로 할게요.)
M: What size do you wear?
(사이즈가 어떻게 되세요?)
G: I wear a small. (작은 사이즈를 입어요.)

3 W: May I help you? (도와드릴까요?)
B: Yes, please. I'm looking for a jacket.
(네. 재킷을 찾고 있어요.)
W: What about this blue jacket?

(이 파란색 재킷 어떠세요?)
B: I like it. Can I try it on?
(마음에 들어요. 입어봐도 될까요?)
W: Sure. What size do you wear?
(그럼요. 사이즈가 어떻게 되세요?)
B: I wear a medium. (중간 사이즈를 입어요.)

P.90~91 **UNIT TEST**

1 ⓐ shirt (셔츠)   ⓑ skirt (치마)
ⓒ pants (바지)   ⓓ shoes (구두)

2 ⓐ They're three dollars. (3달러이다.)
ⓑ They're seven dollars. (7달러이다.)
ⓒ They're thirteen dollars. (13달러이다.)
ⓓ They're fifteen dollars. (15달러이다.)

3 W: May I help you? (도와드릴까요?)
B: Yes. I'm looking for an umbrella.
(네. 우산을 찾고 있어요.)
W: How about this one? (이거 어떠세요?)
B: Oh, I like it! (오, 마음에 들어요!)

4 ⓐ M: May I help you? (도와드릴까요?)
G: Yes, please. I'm looking for a hat.
(네. 모자를 찾고 있어요.)
ⓑ G: How much are these gloves?
(이 장갑 얼마예요?)
M: They're ten dollars. (10달러입니다.)
ⓒ M: What size do you wear?
(사이즈가 어떻게 되세요?)
G: I wear a small. (작은 사이즈를 입어요.)
ⓓ G: Can I try on these shoes?
(이 구두 신어봐도 될까요?)
M: Sure. Go ahead. (그럼요. 그렇게 하세요.)

5 G: Excuse me. I'm looking for a skirt.
(실례합니다. 저는 치마를 찾고 있어요.)
M: What about this one? (이거 어떠세요?)
G: I like it. Can I try it on?
(마음에 들어요. 입어봐도 될까요?)
M: _____
ⓐ Yes, please. (네, 부탁합니다.)
ⓑ It's twelve dollars. (12달러입니다.)
ⓒ Good. I'll take it. (좋아요. 이걸로 할게요.)
ⓓ Sure. What size do you wear?
(그럼요. 사이즈가 어떻게 되세요?)

6 ⓐ W: May I help you? (도와드릴까요?)
B: Yes, please. I'm looking for gloves.
(네. 장갑을 찾고 있어요.)

ⓑ B: How much is this jacket? (이 재킷 얼마예요?)
　W: Fine. I like it. (좋아요. 마음에 들어요.)
ⓒ W: What size do you wear?
　　　 (사이즈가 어떻게 되세요?)
　B: I wear a medium. (중간 사이즈를 입어요.)
ⓓ B: Can I try on these pants?
　　　 (이 바지 입어봐도 될까요?)
　W: Sure. Here they are. (그럼요. 여기 있어요.)

7　B: Mom, I like this blue shirt.
　　　 (엄마, 이 파란색 셔츠가 마음에 들어요.)
　W: Hmm... What about this green one?
　　　 (음… 이 초록색 셔츠는 어떠니?)
　B: Oh, I like it, too. How much is it?
　　　 (오, 이것도 마음에 들어요. 이거 얼마예요?)
　M: It's on sale. It's five dollars.
　　　 (그건 할인 판매 중이에요. 5달러입니다.)
　B: Good. Let's buy it. (좋네요. 이걸로 사요.)

　　Question: Which one will the boy buy?
　　　　　　 (소년은 어느 것을 살 것인가?)

8　W: May I help you? (도와드릴까요?)
　G: Yes. I want this jacket and skirt. How much are
　　　 they? (네. 이 재킷과 치마 주세요. 얼마죠?)
　W: They're fifteen dollars. The jacket is eight
　　　 dollars and the skirt is seven dollars.
　　　 (15달러입니다. 재킷이 8달러이고, 치마가 7달러입니다.)
　G: Okay. I'll take them. (좋아요. 살게요.)

　　Question: How much is the skirt?
　　　　　　 (치마는 얼마인가?)

P.92~93
REVIEW TEST 3　UNITS 7~10

| 1 ⓑ | 2 ⓓ | 3 ⓒ | 4 ⓓ | 5 ⓐ |
| 6 ⓐ | 7 ⓑ | 8 ⓒ | 9 ⓓ | 10 ⓑ |

1　ⓐ wash (씻다)　　ⓑ peel (껍질을 벗기다)
　　ⓒ mix (섞다)　　　ⓓ fry (튀기다)

2　ⓐ dance on a stage (무대 위에서 춤추다)
　　ⓑ watch the fireworks (불꽃놀이를 보다)
　　ⓒ eat snacks (간식을 먹다)
　　ⓓ drink soda (탄산음료를 마시다)

3　G: Do you like to watch movies?
　　　 (너는 영화 보는 것을 좋아하니?)
　B: No, I don't. (아니, 안 좋아해.)
　G: Then, what do you like to do?
　　　 (그럼, 너는 무엇을 하는 것을 좋아하니?)

B: I like to do puzzles. (나는 퍼즐 맞추는 것을 좋아해.)

4　B: Excuse me. I'm looking for a jacket.
　　　 (실례합니다. 저는 재킷을 찾고 있어요.)
　W: What about this blue jacket?
　　　 (이 파란색 재킷은 어떠세요?)
　B: _____
　ⓐ It's ten dollars. (10달러예요.)
　ⓑ What size do you wear? (사이즈가 어떻게 되세요?)
　ⓒ I wear a small. (저는 작은 사이즈를 입어요.)
　ⓓ I like it. Can I try it on?
　　　 (마음에 들어요. 입어봐도 될까요?)

5　B: Where is Kate? (Kate가 어디에 있지?)
　G: She's on the stage. (무대 위에 있어.)
　B: What is she doing there?
　　　 (거기서 무엇을 하고 있는 거니?)
　G: _____
　ⓐ She's singing. (그녀는 노래하고 있어.)
　ⓑ They are dancing very well.
　　　 (그들은 춤을 아주 잘 추고 있어.)
　ⓒ Can I take a photo? (사진 찍어도 되니?)
　ⓓ I'm looking for her. (나는 그녀를 찾고 있어.)

6　ⓐ G: Can I try on this skirt?
　　　　 (이 치마 입어봐도 될까요?)
　　M: Sure. I'll take it. (물론이죠. 이걸로 할게요.)
　ⓑ G: Do you like to take photos?
　　　　 (너는 사진 찍는 것을 좋아하니?)
　　B: Yes, I do. It's my hobby.
　　　　 (응, 좋아해. 그게 내 취미야.)
　ⓒ G: Are they watching the fireworks?
　　　　 (그들은 불꽃놀이를 보고 있니?)
　　B: Yes, they are. (응, 그래.)
　ⓓ G: Will you wash the tomatoes, please?
　　　　 (토마토 좀 씻어줄래?)
　　B: Okay, I will. (응, 그럴게.)

7　ⓐ M: How much are these gloves?
　　　　 (이 장갑 얼마예요?)
　　W: They are eight dollars. (8달러예요.)
　ⓑ M: How does it taste? (맛이 어때요?)
　　W: That's a good idea. (좋은 생각이에요.)
　ⓒ M: What do you like to do on weekends?
　　　　 (주말에 무엇을 하는 것을 좋아하세요?)
　　W: I like to read books.
　　　　 (저는 책 읽는 것을 좋아해요.)
　ⓓ M: What size do you wear?
　　　　 (사이즈가 어떻게 되세요?)
　　W: I wear a medium. (중간 사이즈를 입어요.)

8　M: May I help you? (도와드릴까요?)

G: Yes, please. How much are these pants?
   (네. 이 바지 얼마예요?)
M: They're twelve dollars. (12달러입니다.)
G: How about this skirt? (이 치마는요?)
M: It's on sale. It's seven dollars.
   (그건 할인 판매 중이에요. 7달러입니다.)
G: Good. I'll take it. (좋네요. 이걸로 할게요.)

Question: Which one will the girl buy?
         (소녀는 어느 것을 살 것인가?)

9   B: What are you doing? (너 뭐 하고 있니?)
    G: I'm making soup and salad.
       (수프와 샐러드를 만들고 있어.)
    B: Can I try some soup? (수프 좀 먹어봐도 되니?)
    G: Sure. (pause) How does it taste?
       (물론이지. 맛이 어떠니?)
    B: It's spicy. (매워.)
    G: Do you want to try the salad, too?
       (샐러드도 먹어볼래?)
    B: Yes, please. (pause) Oh, the salad is a little
       sour! (응, 줘. 오, 샐러드는 약간 셔!)

    Question: The soup is spicy and the salad is sour.
             (수프는 맵고 샐러드는 시다.)

10 B: What do you like to do in your free time?
       (너는 여가시간에 무엇을 하는 것을 좋아하니?)
    G: I like to play tennis. (나는 테니스 치는 것을 좋아해.)
    B: Does your brother like to play tennis, too?
       (네 남동생도 테니스 치는 것을 좋아하니?)
    G: No, he doesn't. He likes to listen to music.
       What about you?
       (아니, 안 좋아해. 그는 음악 듣는 것을 좋아해. 너는 어
       때?)
    B: I like to play tennis, too. How about playing
       together after school?
       (나도 테니스 치는 것을 좋아해. 방과 후에 같이 치는 게
       어때?)
    G: That sounds great! (좋아!)

    Question: What does the girl's brother like to
             do?
             (소녀의 남동생은 무엇을 하는 것을 좋아하는
             가?)
    ⓐ He likes to play tennis.
       (그는 테니스 치는 것을 좋아한다.)
    ⓑ He likes to listen to music.
       (그는 음악 듣는 것을 좋아한다.)
    ⓒ He likes to watch movies.
       (그는 영화 보는 것을 좋아한다.)
    ⓓ He likes to play computer games.
       (그는 컴퓨터 게임 하는 것을 좋아한다.)

초등학생의 영어 친구
리스닝버디
LISTENING BUDDY 2

★ 리스닝버디의 특징

- **fun and friendly** 흥미로운 소재로 구성된 쉽고 재미있는 교재
- **step by step** 듣기 실력 향상을 위한 체계적인 구성
- **carefully prepared** 교육부에서 제시한 초등 교과과정의 의사소통 기능 반영
- **authentic language** 실생활에서 활용 가능한 대화 제시
- **productive** 발음 학습 및 speaking 활동을 보강하여 듣기와 말하기의 결합 강화

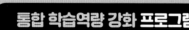

리스닝버디 2

지은이	NE능률 영어교육연구소
연구원	한정은, 백수자, 권혜진, 송진아, 황선영
영문 교열	Peter Morton, MyAn Le, Lewis Hugh Hosie
디자인	방호현, 장현정, 김연주
내지 일러스트	이은교, 전진희, 김현수
내지 사진	www.shutterstock.com
맥편집	ELIM
영업	한기영, 이경구, 박인규, 정철교, 김남준, 김남형, 이우현
마케팅	박혜선, 김여진, 이지원

Let's grow together

NE능률이
미래를
창조합니다.

건강한 배움의 고객가치를 제공하겠다는 꿈을 실현하기 위해
42년 동안 열심히 달려왔습니다.

앞으로도 끊임없는 연구와 노력을 통해
당연한 것을 멈추지 않고

고객, 기업, 직원 모두가 함께 성장하는 NE능률이 되겠습니다.

NE 능률